Busy
Cook's Book

Busy Cook's Book

Anne Ager

TREASURE PRESS

Contents

First published in Great Britain in 1980 by
Sundial Publications Ltd

This edition published in 1984 by
Treasure Press
59 Grosvenor Street
London W1

© Hennerwood Publications Ltd

ISBN 1 85051 003 2

Printed in Hong Kong

INTRODUCTION

The magician that pulls a rabbit out of a hat has nothing on the cook who produces a delicious meal after a busy day's work at the office, or who copes with the numerous family chores and minor crises at home. To pull off such culinary miracles, she must have some tricks up her sleeve, and today there are more ingenious methods of meal preparation than ever before. However, this doesn't mean that she has to rely solely on convenience foods.

This book shows how it is possible to prepare a wide variety of different dishes, using mainly fresh foods, in a very limited space of time.

The greatest secret is to make the maximum use of time when you have it. Use a spare half an hour in the evening to make a sauce. Chop 2 to 3 days' supply of onion, grate oddments of stale cheese, or cook a large batch of rice: they can all be stored in the refrigerator for 2 to 3 days, in the case of cheese slightly longer.

Dishes with strong, characteristic flavours actually benefit from being prepared in advance, so if you have time the night before, choose one of the dishes from the Cook-Ahead section for the following day's dinner. Cover the prepared dishes tightly as pungent flavours, such as curry, quickly spread to other foods in the refrigerator. Many dishes, particularly casseroles, freeze very well, and it's worth making up two while you have the time to spare – one to use immediately, and one to freeze for later use.

Preparing and cooking food quickly

The way that you prepare food prior to cooking can actually save a great deal of time in the kitchen. Chop vegetables, such as onion, as finely as possible; either use one of the chopping gadgets that are now available, or a very sharp knife. Alternatively, you may find it easier to use a coarse grater.

Accompanying vegetables can take as long to cook as the main dish. This cooking time can be reduced by cutting the raw vegetables quite small.

Cube peeled potatoes before boiling them, and treat carrots and other root vegetables in the same way; roughly chop stick beans rather than slicing them; divide cauliflower into small florets, and slice vegetables such as courgettes on a mandolin.

All frozen vegetables can be cooked in under 10 minutes, many under 5. Put sufficient boiling water into the saucepan to give a depth of 2.5 cm/ 1 inch, add salt and the chosen vegetable. Cover the pan and simmer the vegetables quite quickly until they are just tender.

Alternatively, if you are simmering a main dish in a pan on top of the cooker, put the frozen vegetables in a metal sieve or colander over the top of the pan and steam them. Frozen vegetables have a much better texture cooked in this manner, which is a fuel-saver, too.

Make full use of any of the time-saving devices that you have in your kitchen, such as pressure cookers, microwave ovens, electric frying pans and 'slow' cookers. In spite of their name, slow cookers actually can save a great deal of time, as they will cook at a controlled temperature while you are out of the house, so that the meal is ready on your arrival home.

Checklist of handy items for the storecupboard, refrigerator and freezer

Whatever the reason for preparing a meal in a hurry, there are certain standby items that will prove invaluable to the cook who is pushed for time. If you have the following in stock you should never be stumped for a quick meal idea:

Cans
Cream
Custard
Evaporated milk
Fish (tuna, sardines, salmon, etc)
Fruits
Pâté
Soups (including consommé)
Tomatoes

Packets
Biscuits (plain and sweet, e.g. digestive)
Cornflour
Junket/jelly crystals
Pasta
Rice
Stuffing mix
Trifle sponges/sponge fingers

Refrigerator
Cheese (a good cooking variety)
Yogurt

Jars
Honey
Jams
Marmalade
Mayonnaise
Mustard
Pickles

Miscellaneous
Bread mix
Curry powder/paste
Dried fruits
Dried milk
Gelatine
Nuts
Parmesan cheese
Pure lemon/lime juice
Tomato purée

Freezer
Ice cream
Pastry (puff and shortcrust)
Prepared vol-au-vent cases
Vegetables (e.g. peas and sweetcorn)

All the dishes in this book will help you save time spent in the kitchen, and the following general short cuts will save you still further time when cooking:

- Use the blender for quick sauces and soups: liquidize leftover vegetables as the base for a quick soup; liquidize grated cheese, mushrooms and mayonnaise together, in proportions to taste, to make a quick sauce to accompany fish or poultry dishes.
- Ready-prepared sauces can be stored in the refrigerator in screw-top jars for up to 4 days.
- Chop or grate ingredients finely – grated or finely chopped vegetables cook very quickly, as do minced or flaked meats and fish.
- Cooking in a large shallow pan is quicker than using a deep pan.
- Keep frequently used utensils close at hand, not tucked at the back of a cupboard.
- Keep polythene bags of ready-prepared chopped parsley, grated cheese and fresh breadcrumbs in the refrigerator – use within 4 to 5 days.
- Cooking on top of the cooker is generally quicker – if you have the oven on for a main dish, then make the most of it by cooking vegetables in foil parcels in the oven.
- Whenever you use an item from the storecupboard or run out of a certain frequently used ingredient, make a note to replace it.

SNACKS AND SUPPERS

Thirty minutes doesn't seem long in which to prepare a meal, but, with a little thought and imagination there are a number of dishes that can be cooked within half an hour, to serve as a supper or snack. Although quick to prepare they are nevertheless satisfying and nourishing to eat. Some are familiar ideas, such as a variation on Welsh rarebit, others are more unusual like Seafood Spaghetti.

Mushroom and chicken kedgeree

Metric	Imperial
175 g long-grain rice	6 oz long-grain rice
salt	salt
4 eggs	4 eggs
75 g butter	3 oz butter
100 g button mushrooms, sliced	4 oz button mushrooms, sliced
175 g cooked chicken, chopped	6 oz cooked chicken, chopped
4×15 ml spoons double cream	4 tablespoons double cream
freshly ground black pepper	freshly ground black pepper
2×15 ml spoons chopped fresh parsley	2 tablespoons chopped fresh parsley

Preparation and cooking time: 30 minutes

Cook the rice in boiling salted water for about 10 minutes until just tender and drain. Meanwhile, hard-boil, shell and roughly chop the eggs.

Melt the butter in a large shallow pan and add the sliced mushrooms. Cook gently for 3 to 4 minutes, until the mushrooms soften. Add the drained cooked rice, chopped chicken, double cream, chopped hard-boiled egg and salt and pepper to taste. Heat through, then serve sprinkled with chopped parsley.

Creamy sweetcorn chowder

Metric	Imperial
1 medium onion, peeled and finely chopped	1 medium onion, peeled and finely chopped
25 g butter	1 oz butter
3×15 ml spoons plain flour	3 tablespoons plain flour
75 g full fat soft cheese	3 oz full fat soft cheese
300 ml chicken stock	½ pint chicken stock
150 ml milk	¼ pint milk
450 g can sweetcorn kernels	1 lb can sweetcorn kernels
salt	salt
freshly ground black pepper	freshly ground black pepper
150 ml double cream	¼ pint double cream
100 g finely chopped ham or cooked chicken	4 oz finely chopped ham or cooked chicken

Preparation and cooking time: 25 minutes

Fry the onion gently in the butter for 2 minutes. Stir in the flour and cook for 1 minute. Beat in the cheese, then gradually add the stock and milk, whisking to keep the mixture smooth. Add the sweetcorn and salt and pepper to taste, and simmer for 10 minutes. Stir in the cream and heat through gently.

Pour the chowder into warmed soup bowls and sprinkle each portion with a little chopped ham or chicken. Serve with hot crusty bread.

Mushroom and chicken kedgeree;
Creamy sweetcorn chowder

Quick skillet quiche

Metric	Imperial
175 g shortcrust pastry	6 oz shortcrust pastry
3 eggs	3 eggs
300 ml single cream	½ pint single cream
175 g grated cheese	6 oz grated cheese
salt	salt
freshly ground black pepper	freshly ground black pepper
2 large tomatoes, sliced	2 large tomatoes, sliced

Preparation and cooking time: 25 minutes

Roll out the pastry fairly thinly and cut a circle 25 cm (10 inches) in diameter, using a dinner plate as a guide. Line a non-stick omelette pan or frying pan with the pastry, pressing it up the sides well. Prick the base all over with a fork. Put the pan over a gentle heat and cook for 3 to 4 minutes.

Meanwhile, beat the eggs with the cream, two thirds of the cheese, and salt and pepper. Pour this into the pastry case, cover and continue to cook for a further 3 to 4 minutes.

Uncover the pan and top the quiche with the sliced tomato, then sprinkle over the remaining cheese. Put under a preheated hot grill until the filling is puffed and golden. Slide the quiche carefully out of the pan on to a plate to serve.

Tortilla

Metric	Imperial
2×15 ml spoons oil	2 tablespoons oil
1 onion, peeled and thinly sliced	1 onion, peeled and thinly sliced
4 bacon rashers, rinded and chopped	4 bacon rashers, rinded and chopped
2 medium potatoes, cooked and chopped	2 medium potatoes, cooked and chopped
6 eggs	6 eggs
salt	salt
freshly ground black pepper	freshly ground black pepper

Preparation and cooking time: 12 minutes

Heat the oil in a large shallow frying pan, add the onion and bacon and fry for 3 minutes. Add the chopped potatoes and cook for a further minute. Beat the eggs with salt and pepper.

Pour the beaten egg into the pan and cook over a moderate heat for 3 to 4 minutes until set on the underside. Put the pan under a preheated hot grill and cook until the top of the tortilla turns golden. Cut into 4 wedges and serve immediately.

Quick skillet quiche

Tortilla; Pizza omelette

Pizza omelette

Preparation and cooking time: 20 minutes

Metric
8 eggs
salt
freshly ground black pepper
1 large onion, peeled and
 sliced
1 garlic clove, crushed
25 g butter
2×15 ml spoons oil
4 tomatoes, sliced
175 g grated cheese
1 can anchovy fillets
9 black olives

Imperial
8 eggs
salt
freshly ground black pepper
1 large onion, peeled and
 sliced
1 garlic clove, crushed
1 oz butter
2 tablespoons oil
4 tomatoes, sliced
6 oz grated cheese
1 can anchovy fillets
9 black olives

Beat the eggs with salt and pepper. Fry the onion and garlic gently in the butter and oil in a large frying pan or omelette pan for 4 minutes. Add the eggs and cook gently, agitating the egg mixture with a spatula as it cooks and sets.

As soon as the omelette is set on the underside, remove the pan from the heat and arrange the sliced tomatoes on top, then sprinkle over the grated cheese. Put under a preheated hot grill until the cheese is bubbling and golden. Garnish with a criss-cross of anchovy fillets, and the olives. Serve the pizza omelette immediately, cut into wedges.

Variation:
A variety of other ingredients can be used in place of the tomatoes – sliced salami, shredded cooked chicken, sliced mushrooms, flaked sardines, peeled prawns or chopped cooked bacon.

11

Seafood spaghetti; Noodles with bacon; Spaghetti con funghi

Seafood spaghetti

Metric
1 onion, peeled and finely
  chopped
4×15 ml spoons oil
300 ml dry white wine
1 garlic clove, crushed
275 g spaghetti
salt
200 ml double cream
2×15 ml spoons chopped
  chives
175 g peeled prawns
175 g shelled mussels,
  cockles or white crabmeat
freshly ground black pepper

Imperial
1 onion, peeled and finely
  chopped
4 tablespoons oil
½ pint dry white wine
1 garlic clove, crushed
10 oz spaghetti
salt
⅓ pint double cream
2 tablespoons chopped
  chives
6 oz peeled prawns
6 oz shelled mussels, cockles
  or white crabmeat
freshly ground black pepper

Preparation and cooking time: 25 minutes

Fry the chopped onion in 2×15 ml spoons/2 table-spoons of the oil for 2 minutes. Add the white wine and garlic and simmer gently until reduced by one third. Lower the spaghetti into a large pan of boiling salted water and add 1×15 ml spoon/1 tablespoon of the oil. Simmer gently for about 8 minutes until the spaghetti is just tender.
Meanwhile, add the cream, chives, prawns and other shellfish to the reduced wine mixture. Heat through gently and add salt and pepper to taste. Drain the spaghetti well and stir in the remaining oil. Turn on to a hot serving dish and spoon the seafood sauce over the top. Serve immediately.

Noodles with bacon

Metric	Imperial
350 g egg noodles	12 oz egg noodles
3×15 ml spoons oil	3 tablespoons oil
salt	salt
1 onion, peeled and finely chopped	1 onion, peeled and finely chopped
175 g bacon, chopped	6 oz bacon, chopped
4 eggs	4 eggs
freshly ground black pepper	freshly ground black pepper
4×15 ml spoons cream	4 tablespoons cream
chopped fresh parsley, to garnish	chopped fresh parsley, to garnish

Preparation and cooking time: 15 minutes

Put the egg noodles in a large pan of boiling water with 1×15 ml spoon/1 tablespoon of the oil and 1×5 ml spoon/1 teaspoon salt and cook for 6 to 8 minutes, until just tender.

Meanwhile, fry the onion gently in 1×15 ml spoon/1 tablespoon of the oil for 1 to 2 minutes. Add the bacon and fry for a further 2 minutes. Beat the eggs with salt and pepper. Add the eggs to the onion and bacon and cook gently, stirring, until the eggs start to scramble. Remove the pan from the heat.

Drain the cooked noodles and stir in the remaining oil. Turn on to a warmed serving dish. Add the cream to the scrambled egg and heat through for a few seconds. Spoon the egg mixture over the noodles and sprinkle with chopped parsley.

Spaghetti con funghi

Metric	Imperial
1 onion, peeled and finely chopped	1 onion, peeled and finely chopped
4×15 ml spoons oil	4 tablespoons oil
175 g mushrooms, chopped	6 oz mushrooms, chopped
225 g ham, chopped	8 oz ham, chopped
1 garlic clove, crushed	1 garlic clove, crushed
4×15 ml spoons medium sherry	4 tablespoons medium sherry
3×15 ml spoons chopped fresh parsley	3 tablespoons chopped fresh parsley
salt	salt
freshly ground black pepper	freshly ground black pepper
350 g spaghetti	12 oz spaghetti

Preparation and cooking time: 15 minutes

Fry the chopped onion in 2×15 ml spoons/2 tablespoons of the oil for 2 minutes. Add the chopped mushrooms, ham, garlic, sherry, parsley, and salt and pepper. Cover and simmer gently for 10 minutes.

Meanwhile, lower the spaghetti into a large pan of boiling salted water, and add 1×15 ml spoon/1 tablespoon of the oil. Boil gently for about 8 minutes until just tender. Drain the spaghetti well and stir in the remaining oil. Stir the mushroom and ham sauce into the spaghetti and serve immediately.

Variation:
The sherry may be replaced by tomato juice.

Leek and cheese omelette

Metric	Imperial
1 large or 2 medium leeks	*1 large or 2 medium leeks*
50 g butter	*2 oz butter*
6 eggs	*6 eggs*
salt	*salt*
freshly ground black pepper	*freshly ground black pepper*
2×15 ml spoons grated	*2 tablespoons grated*
* Parmesan cheese*	* Parmesan cheese*
100 g full fat soft cheese	*4 oz full fat soft cheese*

Preparation and cooking time: 20 to 25 minutes

Trim and wash the leeks, then shred them quite finely. Melt half the butter in a small saucepan and add the leeks. Cover and simmer gently for 10 minutes.
Beat the eggs with salt and pepper and the Parmesan cheese. Heat the remaining butter in a large omelette pan. Pour in the egg mixture and cook over a moderate heat, agitating the mixture with a spatula as it starts to set, to allow any unset liquid to run under the sides. When the omelette is set on the underside, remove the pan from the heat. Add the warm leek filling and top with small knobs of the cheese. Fold the omelette away from you, and slide it on to a warm plate. Serve immediately.
Serves 2

Leek and cheese omelette

Onion and bacon puffs; Herby sausage patties

Onion and bacon puffs

Metric
1 onion, peeled and finely
 chopped
25 g butter
1×15 ml spoon oil
175 g bacon, rinded and
 chopped
6 eggs, separated
2×15 ml spoons chopped
 fresh parsley
salt
freshly ground black pepper
50 g grated Parmesan cheese

Imperial
1 onion, peeled and finely
 chopped
1 oz butter
1 tablespoon oil
6 oz bacon, rinded and
 chopped
6 eggs, separated
2 tablespoons chopped
 fresh parsley
salt
freshly ground black pepper
2 oz grated Parmesan cheese

Preparation and cooking time: 30 minutes
Oven: 200°C, 400°F, Gas Mark 6

Fry the chopped onion in the butter and oil for 2
minutes. Add the chopped bacon and fry together for
3 minutes. Remove the pan from the heat and beat in
the egg yolks, parsley, and salt and pepper.
Whisk the egg whites until they form stiff peaks. Fold
the egg whites carefully into the onion and bacon
mixture. Spoon into 4 greased individual ovenproof
dishes. Sprinkle the tops with grated Parmesan
cheese. Bake in a preheated oven for 20 minutes.

Herby sausage patties

Metric
450 g pork sausagemeat
1×5 ml spoon mixed dried
 herbs
1×15 ml spoon
 Worcestershire sauce
salt
freshly ground black pepper
oil for frying
4 baps
butter
prepared mustard

Imperial
1 lb pork sausagemeat
1 teaspoon mixed dried
 herbs
1 tablespoon
 Worcestershire sauce
salt
freshly ground black pepper
oil for frying
4 baps
butter
prepared mustard

Preparation and cooking time: 20 minutes

Mix together the sausagemeat, mixed herbs, Worcestershire sauce, and salt and pepper. Form the mixture
into 4 patties. Heat a little oil in a frying pan. Add the
patties and cook for 3 to 4 minutes on one side, then
turn them and cook for a further 4 to 5 minutes until
browned and cooked through.
Meanwhile, split the baps in half and toast the cut
sides. Spread them with butter and a little mustard
and serve each sausage patty between two bap halves.

15

Aubergines and eggs en persillade

Aubergines and eggs en persillade

Metric
1 large aubergine, sliced
oil
6 eggs
salt
freshly ground black pepper
25 g butter
2 garlic cloves, crushed
4 × 15 ml spoons chopped
 fresh parsley
2 × 15 ml spoons sesame
 seeds

Imperial
1 large aubergine, sliced
oil
6 eggs
salt
freshly ground black pepper
1 oz butter
2 garlic cloves, crushed
4 tablespoons chopped fresh
 parsley
2 tablespoons sesame
 seeds

Preparation and cooking time: 25 minutes

Fry the sliced aubergine in a generous amount of oil in a large pan for 3 to 4 minutes on each side, until golden brown and tender. Drain the aubergine thoroughly and put into a hot serving dish and keep warm. Reserve the remaining fat in the pan.
Beat the eggs with salt and pepper. Heat the butter in a heavy saucepan and stir in the beaten eggs. Cook over a gentle heat, stirring continuously, until the eggs scramble and form soft creamy flakes. Spoon the scrambled eggs evenly over the aubergines.
Fry the garlic, chopped parsley and sesame seeds quickly in the fat left from cooking the aubergines. Pour the parsley mixture over the egg and aubergines and serve immediately.

Souffléd rarebits

Metric
25 g butter
1 × 15 ml spoon plain flour
150 ml Guinness
1 × 5 ml spoon prepared
 mustard
225 g grated cheese
2 eggs, separated
salt
freshly ground black pepper
4 slices wholemeal bread
cayenne pepper

Imperial
1 oz butter
1 tablespoon plain flour
¼ pint Guinness
1 teaspoon prepared
 mustard
8 oz grated cheese
2 eggs, separated
salt
freshly ground black pepper
4 slices wholemeal bread
cayenne pepper

Preparation and cooking time: 20 minutes

Melt the butter in a saucepan over a gentle heat. Stir in the flour and cook for 1 minute. Remove the pan from the heat and gradually stir in the Guinness. Bring to the boil gently, stirring until thickened. Add the mustard, grated cheese, egg yolks, and salt and pepper, stirring well. Remove the pan from the heat. Toast the slices of wholemeal bread on one side only.
Whisk the egg whites until they form stiff peaks, and then fold them lightly but thoroughly into the cheese mixture.
Spread a generous amount of the cheese mixture on the untoasted side of each piece of bread, making sure it reaches to the edges of the bread. Put under a preheated moderately hot grill until the cheese topping is golden and bubbling. Sprinkle each rarebit with a little cayenne and serve immediately.

Souffléd rarebits; Macaroni eggs lyonnaise

Macaroni eggs lyonnaise

Metric
225 g shortcut macaroni
oil
salt
25 g butter
1×15 ml spoon plain flour
300 ml milk
4 hard-boiled eggs, chopped
freshly ground black pepper
1 large onion, peeled and
    sliced
75 g grated cheese

Imperial
8 oz shortcut macaroni
oil
salt
1 oz butter
1 tablespoon plain flour
½ pint milk
4 hard-boiled eggs, chopped
freshly ground black pepper
1 large onion, peeled and
    sliced
3 oz grated cheese

Preparation and cooking time: 30 minutes
Oven: 200°C, 400°F, Gas Mark 6

Put the macaroni in a large pan of boiling water with 1×15 ml spoon/1 tablespoon oil and 1×5 ml spoon/ 1 teaspoon salt and cook for 6 minutes.
Meanwhile make the white sauce. Melt the butter in a pan, stir in the flour and cook for 30 seconds. Remove the pan from the heat and gradually stir in the milk. Cook over a gentle heat until thickened. Stir in the chopped hard-boiled eggs and add salt and pepper to taste. Drain the cooked macaroni thoroughly and add to the sauce. Spoon into a lightly oiled ovenproof dish. Fry the sliced onion in a little oil until it starts to brown. Spoon the onion over the macaroni and sprinkle with the grated cheese. Bake in the oven for 15 minutes. Serve immediately with a tomato salad.

Ham scramble

Metric	Imperial
2 baps, halved	2 baps, halved
6 eggs	6 eggs
2×15 ml spoons grated Parmesan cheese	2 tablespoons grated Parmesan cheese
salt	salt
freshly ground black pepper	freshly ground black pepper
75 g butter	3 oz butter
100 g lean ham, chopped	4 oz lean ham, chopped
2×15 ml spoons double cream	2 tablespoons double cream
cayenne pepper	cayenne pepper

Preparation and cooking time: 15 minutes

Toast the baps cut side uppermost. Turn off the grill and leave the baps under it to keep warm. Beat the eggs with the Parmesan cheese and salt and pepper. Melt 25 g (1 oz) of the butter in a non-stick saucepan. Add the egg mixture and cook over a gentle heat, stirring constantly with a wooden spoon, until the mixture forms soft creamy flakes. Remove the saucepan from the heat and stir in the ham and cream. Stir over the heat for 1 to 2 minutes.
Spread the toasted bap halves with the remaining butter and top each with the scrambled egg and ham. Sprinkle each topping with a little cayenne pepper and serve immediately.

Variation:
Use 175 g (6 oz) flaked cooked kipper fillet in place of the ham, and omit the Parmesan cheese.

Mushroom and bacon toasts

Metric	Imperial
75 g butter	3 oz butter
6 bacon rashers, rinded and chopped	6 bacon rashers, rinded and chopped
225 g button mushrooms, cleaned	8 oz button mushrooms, cleaned
1×15 ml spoon chopped fresh parsley	1 tablespoon chopped fresh parsley
salt	salt
freshly ground black pepper	freshly ground black pepper
8 thin slices bread	8 thin slices bread
100 g full fat soft cheese	4 oz full fat soft cheese

Preparation and cooking time: 15 minutes

Melt half the butter in a shallow pan, add the chopped bacon and fry for 2 to 3 minutes. Add the mushrooms, parsley, and salt and pepper. Cover the pan and cook gently for 6 to 8 minutes or until the mushrooms are just tender.
Meanwhile toast the bread on both sides. Spread four of the slices on one side with the remaining butter and the cream cheese. Sandwich together in pairs with the remaining slices of toast. Spoon the hot mushrooms and bacon over the top.

From left: Ham scramble;
Mushroom and bacon toasts;
Creamed chicken livers

Creamed chicken livers

Metric
50 g butter
1 onion, peeled and finely
   chopped
350 g chicken livers
salt
freshly ground black pepper
4 × 15 ml spoons soured
   cream
1 egg yolk
4 breakfast rusks

Imperial
2 oz butter
1 onion, peeled and finely
   chopped
12 oz chicken livers
salt
freshly ground black pepper
4 tablespoons soured
   cream
1 egg yolk
4 breakfast rusks

Preparation and cooking time: 12 minutes

Heat the butter in a frying pan, add the chopped onions and fry gently for 2 to 3 minutes. Add the chicken livers and cook gently, stirring occasionally, until the outsides are sealed. Add salt and pepper. Blend the soured cream with the egg yolk and stir it into the chicken livers. Stir over the heat for 2 minutes, then spoon on to the breakfast rusks and serve immediately.

Pipérade with black pudding

Metric	Imperial
3 × 15 ml spoons oil	3 tablespoons oil
1 onion, very thinly sliced	1 onion, very thinly sliced
1 garlic clove, crushed (optional)	1 garlic clove, crushed (optional)
175 g black pudding, cut into rings	6 oz black pudding, cut into rings
1 green pepper, cored, seeded and very thinly sliced	1 green pepper, cored, seeded and very thinly sliced
6 large tomatoes, roughly chopped	6 large tomatoes, roughly chopped
4 eggs	4 eggs
1 × 5 ml spoon dried basil	1 teaspoon dried basil
salt	salt
freshly ground black pepper	freshly ground black pepper

Preparation and cooking time: 15 minutes

The inclusion of black pudding turns the usual pipérade mixture of vegetables into a more substantial dish, but it can be omitted.

Heat the oil in a frying pan, add the onion and fry gently for 2 minutes. Add the garlic (if using), black pudding, green pepper and tomatoes and cook together gently for 5 minutes.
Beat the eggs with the basil, and salt and pepper. Add the eggs to the pan and stir over a gentle heat until the mixture begins to thicken like scrambled egg. Remove from the heat and serve immediately.

Pipérade with black pudding

Smoked haddock in lemon butter sauce

Metric	Imperial
750 g smoked haddock fillet	1½ lb smoked haddock fillet
300 ml milk	½ pint milk
grated rind of 1 lemon	grated rind of 1 lemon
salt	salt
freshly ground black pepper	freshly ground black pepper
4 slices white bread	4 slices white bread
2 × 5 ml spoons cornflour	2 teaspoons cornflour
25 g butter	1 oz butter
lemon slices, to garnish	lemon slices, to garnish

Preparation and cooking time: 20 minutes

Cut the smoked haddock fillet into four equal portions and put into a shallow pan with the milk, lemon rind, and salt and pepper. Cover the pan and simmer gently for 8 to 10 minutes. Meanwhile toast the bread on both sides. Remove the crusts and cut the toast into triangles.
Blend the cornflour to a paste with a little water. Remove the cooked fish from the pan using a fish slice and put on to a warmed serving dish.
Stir the blended cornflour into the fish cooking liquid and bring to the boil, stirring, until thickened. Stir in the butter. Spoon the sauce over the fish, garnish with lemon slices and serve with toast triangles.

Smoked haddock in lemon butter sauce; Potted fish

Potted fish

Metric
350 g smoked haddock,
    flaked
pinch of grated nutmeg
150 ml single cream
salt
freshly ground black pepper
50 g butter

Imperial
12 oz smoked haddock,
    flaked
pinch of grated nutmeg
¼ pint single cream
salt
freshly ground black pepper
2 oz butter

Preparation and cooking time: 20 minutes
Oven: 200°C, 400°F, Gas Mark 6

Mix the flaked fish with the nutmeg, cream, and salt
and pepper. Spoon the mixture into 4 cocotte or small
ovenproof dishes. Dot the surfaces with small knobs of
the butter.
Stand the dishes in a roasting tin and add sufficient
boiling water to come half way up the sides of the
dishes. Bake in a preheated oven for 12 to 15 minutes
until golden.
Alternatively, stand the dishes in a shallow pan containing a little boiling water. Cover the pan and
simmer gently for 12 to 15 minutes.
Serve at once.

21

Vegetable soufflé

Metric	Imperial
225 g cooked potatoes	½ lb cooked potatoes
225 g cooked cauliflower, carrot, swede, parsnips or Brussels sprouts (or a mixture)	½ lb cooked cauliflower, carrot, swede, parsnips or Brussels sprouts (or a mixture)
4 × 15 ml spoons single cream	4 tablespoons single cream
3 eggs, separated	3 eggs, separated
100 g grated cheese	4 oz grated cheese
salt	salt
freshly ground black pepper	freshly ground black pepper

Vegetable soufflé; Mustard eggs

Preparation and cooking time: 30 minutes
Oven: 220°C, 425°F, Gas Mark 7

Avoid opening the oven door whilst the soufflé is rising, or it will sink at once.

Mash the cooked potatoes with the other cooked vegetables, then beat in the cream, egg yolks, grated cheese, and salt and pepper.
Whisk the egg whites until stiff, then fold them lightly but thoroughly into the vegetable mixture. Spoon the mixture into a greased 18 cm (7 inch) soufflé dish or round deep ovenproof dish. Bake in a preheated oven for 20 minutes until well risen and lightly coloured on top. Serve immediately with a mixed salad.

Mustard eggs

Metric	Imperial
50 g butter	2 oz butter
8 eggs	8 eggs
salt	salt
freshly ground black pepper	freshly ground black pepper
150 ml soured cream	¼ pint soured cream
2 × 5 ml spoons French mustard	2 teaspoons French mustard
fresh parsley, to garnish	fresh parsley, to garnish
fingers of toast or brown bread and butter, to serve	fingers of toast or brown bread and butter, to serve

Preparation and cooking time: 20 minutes
Oven: 190°C, 375°F, Gas Mark 5

Put a generous knob of butter into the base of 4 cocotte or small ovenproof dishes. Put into a preheated oven for 2 minutes to melt the butter.
Carefully crack 2 eggs into each dish and add salt and pepper. Return the dishes to the oven and cook the eggs for 8 to 10 minutes, until just set.
Mix the soured cream with the French mustard and spoon the flavoured cream evenly over the eggs. Return the eggs to the oven for 2 minutes. Serve hot with fingers of toast or brown bread and butter and garnished with chopped parsley.

MAIN DISHES

Most cooks have to plan at least one main meal a day, sometimes two. It's quite a problem to think of something that is both nourishing and quick to prepare, at the same time ringing the changes from day to day. All of the following main dishes can be prepared and cooked within an hour, including the cooking of any accompanying vegetables.

Spanish mince

Metric	Imperial
1 medium onion, peeled and thinly sliced	1 medium onion, peeled and thinly sliced
2 × 15 ml spoons oil	2 tablespoons oil
2 garlic cloves, crushed	2 garlic cloves, crushed
500 g minced beef	1¼ lb minced beef
2 eating apples, grated	2 eating apples, grated
50 g raisins	2 oz raisins
300 ml beef stock	½ pint beef stock
75 g stuffed olives	3 oz stuffed olives
coarsely grated rind of 1 orange	coarsely grated rind of 1 orange
salt	salt
freshly ground black pepper	freshly ground black pepper

Preparation and cooking time: 40 minutes

Fry the onion in the oil in a large shallow pan for 2 minutes. Add the garlic and the mince and cook until lightly browned. Stir in the grated apple, raisins and beef stock. Cover the pan and simmer gently for 20 minutes. Thickly slice the stuffed olives and stir in with the grated orange rind, and salt and pepper to taste. Simmer for a further 10 minutes.
Serve with hot crusty bread and a mixed salad.

Country liver sauté

Metric	Imperial
2 medium onions, peeled and sliced	2 medium onions, peeled and sliced
3 × 15 ml spoons oil	3 tablespoons oil
750 g pig's liver, cut into 2.5 cm squares	1½ lb pig's liver, cut into 1 inch squares
seasoned flour	seasoned flour
450 ml chicken stock	¾ pint chicken stock
150 ml tomato juice	¼ pint tomato juice
4 celery sticks, chopped	4 celery sticks chopped
4 medium courgettes, sliced	4 medium courgettes, sliced
1 bay leaf	1 bay leaf
salt	salt
freshly ground black pepper	freshly ground black pepper

Preparation and cooking time: 1 hour

Fry the sliced onions in the oil in a large shallow pan for 3 minutes. Dust the pieces of liver in the seasoned flour, and add them to the pan.
Continue frying until the liver is lightly coloured on all sides, then gradually stir in the chicken stock. Add the tomato juice, celery, courgettes, bay leaf, and salt and pepper to taste. Cover and simmer for 45 minutes.
Remove the bay leaf before serving, and serve with cooked noodles or rice, and a tomato salad.
Vegetable tip: cook the noodles or rice while the liver is simmering.

Veal with orange

Metric	Imperial
2 large oranges	2 large oranges
4 veal escalopes, flattened	4 veal escalopes, flattened
seasoned flour	seasoned flour
50 g butter	2 oz butter
150 ml single cream	¼ pint single cream
salt	salt
freshly ground black pepper	freshly ground black pepper

Preparation and cooking time: 45 minutes

Coarsely grate the rind and squeeze the juice from 1 of the oranges. Peel the remaining orange, removing the pith, and divide into segments. Place the peel and segments on one side for garnishing. Dust the veal escalopes in seasoned flour.
Heat the butter in a large shallow pan. Add the veal escalopes and fry gently for 4 to 5 minutes. Turn the escalopes and fry for a further 4 to 5 minutes. Add the orange juice and grated rind and boil rapidly for 1 minute. Stir in the cream, and salt and pepper to taste. Heat through without boiling.
Serve the veal escalopes garnished with orange segments and thin strips of orange peel. Serve with new potatoes and peas.
Vegetable tip: start cooking the new potatoes just before you fry the escalopes. Cook frozen green peas while you finish the orange sauce.

Spanish mince; Country liver sauté; Veal with orange

Rabbit and onion casserole

Rabbit and onion casserole

Metric
2 medium onions, peeled
   and sliced
3 × 15 ml spoons oil
8 small rabbit joints
seasoned flour
1 × 15 ml spoon French
   mustard
1 × 15 ml spoon demerara
   sugar
600 ml chicken stock
1 bay leaf
4 slices French bread
50 g Cheddar cheese, grated
1 × 15 ml spoon chopped
   fresh parsley

Imperial
2 medium onions, peeled
   and sliced
3 tablespoons oil
8 small rabbit joints
seasoned flour
1 tablespoon French
   mustard
1 tablespoon demerara
   sugar
1 pint chicken stock
1 bay leaf
4 slices French bread
2 oz Cheddar cheese, grated
1 tablespoon chopped
   fresh parsley

Preparation and cooking time: 1 hour
Oven temperature: 190°C, 373°F, Gas Mark 5

Fry the onions in the oil for 2 to 3 minutes. Dust the rabbit joints in the seasoned flour. Add the rabbit joints to the pan and fry until lightly browned on all sides. Add the French mustard, demerara sugar, chicken stock and bay leaf, and bring to the boil. Transfer to a casserole, cover and cook in a preheated oven for 40 minutes.

Uncover the casserole, top the rabbit and onion with the slices of French bread, sprinkle with grated cheese, then return the uncovered casserole to the oven for a further 5 minutes.

Sprinkle with chopped fresh parsley and serve with Brussels sprouts and boiled potatoes.

Vegetable tip: cut the peeled potatoes into cubes.

Cook the potatoes and the sprouts for 15 minutes so that they are ready at the same time as the rabbit.

Chicken in mushroom sauce

Metric	Imperial
4 chicken joints	4 chicken joints
2×15 ml spoons oil	2 tablespoons oil
175 g button mushrooms, sliced	6 oz button mushrooms, sliced
1×15 ml spoon plain flour	1 tablespoon plain flour
300 ml white wine	½ pint white wine
150 ml chicken stock	¼ pint chicken stock
150 ml soured cream	¼ pint soured cream
pinch of grated nutmeg	pinch of grated nutmeg
salt	salt
freshly ground black pepper	freshly ground black pepper

Preparation and cooking time: 1 hour

Fry the chicken joints in the oil in a large shallow pan until brown on all sides. Add the mushrooms and fry with the chicken for 1 minute.

Stir in the flour, then gradually add the wine, stock, soured cream, nutmeg, and salt and pepper. Cover the pan and simmer gently for about 45 minutes until the chicken is tender. Serve with plain boiled rice and a tossed green salad.

Vegetable tip: start cooking the rice 15 minutes before the chicken is due to be ready. Drain the rice and return it to the pan with a generous knob of butter.

Chicken and rice hotpot

Metric	Imperial
2 medium onions, peeled and finely chopped	2 medium onions, peeled and finely chopped
3×15 ml spoons oil	3 tablespoons oil
4 chicken drumsticks	4 chicken drumsticks
175 g long-grain rice	6 oz long-grain rice
600 ml chicken stock	1 pint chicken stock
225 g carrots, peeled and thinly sliced	8 oz carrots, peeled and thinly sliced
1 bay leaf	1 bay leaf
salt	salt
freshly ground black pepper	freshly ground black pepper

Preparation and cooking time: 50 minutes

Fry the onions gently in the oil for 3 minutes. Add the chicken drumsticks to the pan and fry them until lightly browned on all sides. Add the rice and cook for 1 minute, stirring continuously.

Stir in the chicken stock, carrots, bay leaf, and salt and pepper. Simmer gently, covered, for 35 to 40 minutes, until the chicken is tender.

Serve with a tomato and onion salad.

Chicken in mushroom sauce; Chicken and rice hotpot

Plaice and onion mornay

Metric
2 onions, peeled and thinly
  sliced
25 g butter
8 plaice fillets
salt
freshly ground black pepper
grated rind of 1 lemon
4×15 ml spoons chopped
  fresh parsley
300 ml dry white wine
2 egg yolks
4×15 ml spoons double
  cream
1×5 ml spoon cornflour
pinch of grated nutmeg
100 g Gruyère cheese, grated

Imperial
2 onions, peeled and thinly
  sliced
1 oz butter
8 plaice fillets
salt
freshly ground black pepper
grated rind of 1 lemon
4 tablespoons chopped
  fresh parsley
½ pint dry white wine
2 egg yolks
4 tablespoons double
  cream
1 teaspoon cornflour
pinch of grated nutmeg
4 oz Gruyère cheese, grated

Preparation and cooking time: 45 minutes

Fry the onions very gently in the butter in a large shallow pan for 8 minutes. Meanwhile, season the plaice fillets with salt and pepper and sprinkle with the lemon rind and parsley. Roll up the plaice fillets.

Arrange the fillets on top of the onion in the pan and pour over the wine. Cover with a lid or a circle of greased greaseproof paper and simmer gently for 8 to 10 minutes, until the fish is tender.

Carefully remove the cooked fish and the onion to a heated ovenproof dish, using a fish slice. Beat the egg yolks with the cream and the cornflour, then blend in the fish poaching liquid. Pour the mixture into the shallow pan and stir over a gentle heat until the sauce thickens. Stir in the grated nutmeg and half of the grated cheese.

Spoon the sauce over the fish and onion and sprinkle with the remaining cheese. Brown under a preheated hot grill.

Serve with buttered courgettes and sauté potatoes.

Vegetable tip: start cooking the sliced courgettes 15 minutes before the fish is due to be ready to serve. Slice leftover cooked potatoes and fry them in a mixture of oil and melted butter while the fish is browning under the grill.

Stuffed mackerel with orange and parsley

Metric
6 ×15 ml spoons fresh white
    breadcrumbs
grated rind of 2 oranges
1 ×15 ml spoon clear honey
3 ×15 ml spoons chopped
    fresh parsley
1 egg, beaten
salt
freshly ground black pepper
3 ×15 ml spoons marmalade
juice of ½ lemon
4 medium mackerel, cleaned
oil

Imperial
6 tablespoons fresh white
    breadcrumbs
grated rind of 2 oranges
1 tablespoon clear honey
3 tablespoons chopped
    fresh parsley
1 egg, beaten
salt
freshly ground black pepper
3 tablespoons marmalade
juice of ½ lemon
4 medium mackerel, cleaned
oil

Preparation and cooking time: 1 hour
Oven temperature: 190°C, 375°F, Gas Mark 5

Mix the breadcrumbs with the grated orange rind, honey, parsley, beaten egg, and salt and pepper. Heat the marmalade with the lemon juice until dissolved. Stuff the mackerel with the orange and breadcrumb stuffing.
Place the fish in a large greased shallow ovenproof dish. Brush the fish with a little oil, spoon over the marmalade glaze. Bake in a preheated oven for 35 to 40 minutes.
Serve with sauté potatoes and a chicory and watercress or mixed salad.
Vegetable tip: Use leftover cooked potatoes – fry them in melted butter or oil just before the fish is ready.

Plaice and onion mornay;
Stuffed mackerel with orange and parsley

29

Deep dish cod pie

Preparation and cooking time: 1 hour
Oven temperature: 190°C, 375°F, Gas Mark 5

Metric
50 g butter
3×15 ml spoons plain flour
450 ml milk
500 g cod fillet. cubed
pinch of grated nutmeg
salt
freshly ground black pepper
2 hard-boiled eggs, sliced
4 medium potatoes, very
    thinly sliced
2×15 ml spoons melted
    butter
2×15 ml spoons dried
    breadcrumbs

Imperial
2 oz butter
3 tablespoons plain flour
¾ pint milk
1¼ lb cod fillet, cubed
pinch of grated nutmeg
salt
freshly ground black pepper
2 hard-boiled eggs, sliced
4 medium potatoes, very
    thinly sliced
2 tablespoons melted
    butter
2 tablespoons dried
    breadcrumbs

Melt the butter in a pan. Stir in the flour and cook for 1 minute. Remove the pan from the heat and gradually stir in the milk. Bring to the boil, stirring until thickened. Add the cubed cod, nutmeg, and salt and pepper to taste. Simmer for 2 to 3 minutes.

Put half the fish mixture into a greased deep ovenproof dish, 20 cm/8 inches in diameter. Top with the sliced hard-boiled egg and then the remaining fish mixture. Cover with overlapping slices of potato. Brush with the melted butter and sprinkle with the dried breadcrumbs. Bake the pie in a preheated oven for 35 to 40 minutes.

Serve with a tomato salad and a green vegetable.

Hake in red wine

Metric
1 hake (about 1.25 kg)
2 onions, peeled and sliced
50 g butter
4 bacon rashers, rinded and
 chopped
1 green pepper, cored,
 seeded and sliced
1 garlic clove, crushed
 (optional)
300 ml red wine
1 bay leaf
salt
freshly ground black pepper
2 × 5 ml spoons cornflour

Imperial
1 hake (about 2½ lb)
2 onions, peeled and sliced
2 oz butter
4 bacon rashers, rinded and
 chopped
1 green pepper, cored,
 seeded and sliced
1 garlic clove, crushed
 (optional)
½ pint red wine
1 bay leaf
salt
freshly ground black pepper
2 teaspoons cornflour

Preparation and cooking time: 1 hour

Cut the head and tail off the fish, and clean the inside.
Cut the body of the fish into slices about 4 cm/1½
inches thick.
Fry the onions gently in the butter for 2 minutes, then
add the bacon and fry for a further minute. Add the
green pepper, garlic, red wine, bay leaf, and salt and
pepper. Blend the cornflour with a little cold water to
make a smooth paste and add to the contents of the
pan, stirring well.
Bring the mixture to the boil, simmer for 3 minutes,
then add the pieces of hake. Cover the pan and simmer
gently for 30 minutes.
Serve with plain boiled potatoes and a green vegetable
such as peas. Cook the vegetables while the fish is
simmering.

Baked mullet with potatoes and olives

Metric
450 g potatoes, peeled and
 very thinly sliced
75 g butter
4 red mullet, cleaned
4 lemon slices
100 g pitted black olives
4 sprigs fresh dill or fennel or
 2 × 5 ml spoons dried dill
 or fennel
salt
freshly ground black pepper
olive oil

Imperial
1 lb potatoes, peeled and
 very thinly sliced
3 oz butter
4 red mullet, cleaned
4 lemon slices
4 oz pitted black olives
4 sprigs fresh dill or fennel or
 2 teaspoons dried dill or
 fennel
salt
freshly ground black pepper
olive oil

Preparation and cooking time: 1 hour
Oven temperature: 190°C, 375°F, Gas Mark 5

Arrange the potatoes in a layer in the base of a greased
shallow ovenproof dish and dot with knobs of the
butter. Stuff each mullet with a slice of lemon, 2
olives, and a sprig or pinch of dried dill or fennel.
Place the stuffed mullet on top of the potatoes. Add
salt and pepper and scatter over the remaining olives.
Sprinkle the fish generously with oil and bake in a
preheated oven for 35 minutes.
Serve with a cucumber salad.

Left from front: Hake in red wine; Deep dish cod pie
Right: Baked mullet with potatoes and olives

Pork fillet with peanut sauce

Metric
500 g pork fillet, cut into
small round slices
seasoned flour
50 g butter
1 medium onion, peeled and
finely chopped
3×15 ml spoons smooth
peanut butter
450 ml hot chicken stock
salt
freshly ground black pepper
50 g salted peanuts
(optional)

Imperial
1¼ lb pork fillet, cut into
small round slices
seasoned flour
2 oz butter
1 medium onion, peeled and
finely chopped
3 tablespoons smooth
peanut butter
¾ pint hot chicken stock
salt
freshly ground black pepper
2 oz salted peanuts
(optional)

Preparation time: 35 to 40 minutes

Dust the pork slices in the seasoned flour. Heat the butter in a large shallow pan, add the chopped onion and fry gently until the onion begins to colour. Add the pork slices and cook until they are lightly browned on all sides.

Blend the peanut butter with the hot stock and stir into the pan with salt and pepper to taste. Cover the pan and simmer for about 20 minutes until the pork is tender. Sprinkle with salted peanuts and serve with broccoli and boiled noodles.

Vegetable tip: put the broccoli on to cook at the same time as you cover the pork to simmer for 20 minutes. Cook noodles in boiling salted water for 8 to 10 minutes, just before the pork is cooked. Drain the noodles and toss them in melted butter.

Piquant pork spare ribs

Metric	Imperial
4 pieces pork spare rib	4 pieces pork spare rib
1 × 15 ml spoon French mustard	1 tablespoon French mustard
2 × 15 ml spoons Worcestershire sauce	2 tablespoons Worcestershire sauce
2 × 15 ml spoons demerara sugar	2 tablespoons demerara sugar
grated rind and juice of 1 lemon	grated rind and juice of 1 lemon
1 × 5 ml spoon curry powder	1 teaspoon curry powder
1 garlic clove, crushed	1 garlic clove, crushed
2 × 15 ml spoons oil	2 tablespoons oil
salt	salt
freshly ground black pepper	freshly ground black pepper
2 × 15 ml spoons finely chopped gherkin	2 tablespoons finely chopped gherkin
2 × 15 ml spoons finely chopped red pepper	2 tablespoons finely chopped red pepper

Preparation and cooking time: 45 to 50 minutes
Oven temperature: 200°C, 400°F, Gas Mark 6

Use the meaty (English) pork spare rib, not the Chinese cut. The pieces should weigh approximately 175 g (6 oz) each.

Pierce the pieces of pork spare rib all over with a fine skewer. Mix together the French mustard, Worcestershire sauce, demerara sugar, lemon rind and juice, curry powder, garlic, oil, and salt and pepper.
Put the pork spare rib into a shallow ovenproof dish and spread the mixture evenly over the meat. Cook in a preheated oven for 35 to 40 minutes, until glazed to a golden brown and the meat is tender. Sprinkle with the chopped gherkin and red pepper and serve with chips and a cucumber and yogurt salad.
Vegetable tip: use frozen chips for quickness – to save heating a pan of deep fat or oil, spread the frozen chips out on an oiled baking sheet and cook for 20 to 25 minutes in the oven with the pork.

From front: Piquant pork spare ribs;
Pork fillet with peanut sauce

Savoury pork loaf with barbecue sauce

Metric
1 medium onion, peeled and
    grated
450 g lean pork, minced
75 g fresh breadcrumbs
3×15 ml spoons apple sauce
    or purée
1×2.5 ml spoon dried sage
salt
freshly ground black pepper
1 egg

Barbecue sauce:
150 ml dry cider
2×15 ml spoons vinegar
1×15 ml spoon tomato
    purée
3×15 ml spoons chutney
1×15 ml spoon
    Worcestershire sauce
2×5 ml spoons French
    mustard
2×15 ml spoons brown
    sugar
1 garlic clove, crushed

Imperial
1 medium onion, peeled and
    grated
1 lb lean pork, minced
3 oz fresh breadcrumbs
3 tablespoons apple sauce or
    purée
½ teaspoon dried sage
salt
freshly ground black pepper
1 egg

Barbecue sauce:
¼ pint dry cider
2 tablespoons vinegar
1 tablespoon tomato
    purée
3 tablespoons chutney
1 tablespoon
    Worcestershire sauce
2 teaspoons French
    mustard
2 tablespoons brown
    sugar
1 garlic clove, crushed

Preparation and cooking time: 1 hour
Oven: 200°C, 400°F, Gas Mark 6

Mix together the ingredients for the loaf. Press the mixture into a well greased 450 g (1 lb) loaf tin. Bake in the oven for 50 minutes. Meanwhile make the sauce. Put all the sauce ingredients into a pan, adding salt and pepper, then simmer for 5 minutes.

Unmould the hot loaf on to a serving platter. Serve cut in slices, with the barbecue sauce, mashed potato, and green beans.

Vegetable tip: cut the peeled potatoes into small pieces so that they cook quickly. Cook the potatoes and the beans for the last 20 minutes that the meat loaf is in the oven. Drain and mash the potatoes.

Pork chops with cranberry

Preparation and cooking time: 1 hour
Oven: 180°C, 350°F, Gas Mark 4

Metric	Imperial
1 small red cabbage, finely shredded	1 small red cabbage, finely shredded
1 medium onion, peeled and thinly sliced	1 medium onion, peeled and thinly sliced
4 cloves	4 cloves
1 eating apple, cored and sliced	1 eating apple, cored and sliced
4×15 ml spoons red wine vinegar	4 tablespoons red wine vinegar
4×15 ml spoons demerara sugar	4 tablespoons demerara sugar
salt	salt
freshly ground black pepper	freshly ground black pepper
4 pork chops	4 pork chops
2×15 ml spoons oil	2 tablespoons oil
150 ml red wine	¼ pint red wine
4×15 ml spoons cranberry sauce	4 tablespoons cranberry sauce
grated rind of 1 orange	grated rind of 1 orange

Put the shredded red cabbage, onion, cloves, apple, red wine vinegar, sugar, and salt and pepper into a casserole. Cover and cook in a preheated moderate oven for 1 hour.

Fry the pork chops on both sides in the oil until lightly browned. Add the red wine, cranberry sauce, orange rind and salt and pepper. Cover and simmer gently for about 40 minutes until the pork chops are tender and glazed. Serve the pork chops accompanied by the cooked red cabbage.

Note: If the pork chops are ready some time before the cabbage is cooked, add the chops and their sauce to the casserole and finish cooking together.

Savoury pork loaf with barbecue sauce;
Pork chops with cranberry

Salmon and watercress roll

Metric
2 bunches watercress
200 g can salmon
3×15 ml spoons plain flour
grated rind of ½ lemon
100 g full fat soft cheese
150 g single cream
3 eggs, separated
salt
freshly ground black pepper
4×15 ml spoons thick
   mayonnaise
1 lemon, quartered, to serve

Imperial
2 bunches watercress
7 oz can salmon
3 tablespoons plain flour
grated rind of ½ lemon
4 oz full fat soft cheese
¼ pint single cream
3 eggs, separated
salt
freshly ground black pepper
4 tablespoons thick
   mayonnaise
1 lemon, quartered, to serve

Preparation and cooking time: 50 minutes
Oven: 180°C, 350°F, Gas Mark 4

Wash the watercress and remove the leaves in sprigs, discarding the tough stalks. Reserve a few sprigs for garnish. Put the remaining watercress leaves into the liquidizer with the salmon, flour, lemon rind, cheese, cream, egg yolks, and salt and pepper to taste. Blend until smooth, then pour into a bowl.

Whisk the egg whites until they will form soft peaks, then fold them into the salmon mixture. Spread the mixture evenly into a greased and lined shallow tin, approximately 25×18 cm/10×7 inches. Bake in a preheated oven for 25 minutes, until spongy but firm to the touch.

Turn out immediately on to a damp clean cloth, and remove the lining paper. Spread the 'sponge' with mayonnaise and roll up as for a Swiss roll. Transfer to a warm serving dish and garnish with the reserved watercress and the lemon quarters. Serve with new potatoes and peas.

Vegetable tip: use frozen peas for speed. Cook the scraped new potatoes slowly in butter, when you put the salmon and watercress roll into the oven.

Clockwise from top right: Egg plant creole;
Egg and sweetcorn fricassée; Salmon and watercress roll

Egg plant creole

Metric
4 small aubergines
4×15 ml spoons oil
salt
1 medium onion, peeled and
   chopped
100 g mushrooms, chopped
1 garlic clove, crushed
175 g ham, finely chopped
1×5 ml spoon curry powder
freshly ground black pepper
2×15 ml spoons tomato
   purée
1×15 ml spoon
   Worcestershire sauce

Imperial
4 small aubergines
4 tablespoons oil
salt
1 medium onion, peeled and
   chopped
4 oz mushrooms, chopped
1 garlic clove, crushed
6 oz ham, finely chopped
1 teaspoon curry powder
freshly ground black pepper
2 tablespoons tomato
   purée
1 tablespoon
   Worcestershire sauce

Preparation and cooking time: 1 hour
Oven temperature: 190°C, 375°F, Gas Mark 5

Cut the aubergines in half lengthways. Score the cut surfaces at regular intervals with a sharp knife, making sure that the point of the knife does not go through the skin of the aubergines. Rub the scored surfaces with oil and salt, then place the aubergine halves, cut sides uppermost, on a greased baking sheet. Bake in a preheated oven for 15 minutes.
Remove the aubergines from the oven. Scoop the flesh into a bowl using a grapefruit spoon or teaspoon. Fry the onion and mushrooms in 3×15 ml spoons/3 tablespoons oil for 3 minutes. Add the garlic and aubergines flesh and fry together, stirring, for a further 2 minutes. Add the ham, curry powder, tomato purée, Worcestershire sauce, and salt and pepper to taste.
Fill the aubergine 'shells' with the ham mixture and place back on the baking sheet. Sprinkle with a little oil, and bake in the oven for 25 to 30 minutes.
Serve hot with a mixed salad.

Egg and sweetcorn fricassée

Metric
8 eggs
50 g butter
3×15 ml spoons plain flour
300 ml chicken stock
300 ml milk
275 g canned sweetcorn
   kernels
6×15 ml spoons cooked peas
salt
freshly ground black pepper
2×15 ml spoons chopped
   fresh parsley

Imperial
8 eggs
2 oz butter
3 tablespoons plain flour
½ pint chicken stock
½ pint milk
10 oz canned sweetcorn
   kernels
6 tablespoons cooked peas
salt
freshly ground black pepper
2 tablespoons chopped
   fresh parsley

To serve:
fingers of hot toast
boiled rice

To serve:
fingers of hot toast
boiled rice

Preparation and cooking time: 20 minutes

Put the eggs into a pan of cold water, heat and gently boil for 4 minutes. Drain and then rinse the eggs in cold water. Carefully remove the shells and put the eggs into a bowl of warm water. Melt the butter in a saucepan. Stir in the flour and cook for 1 minute. Remove the pan from the heat and gradually stir in the chicken stock and milk. Bring to the boil and add the sweetcorn kernels, peas, soft-boiled eggs, and salt and pepper to taste. Simmer together for 2 to 3 minutes.
Serve the egg and sweetcorn fricassée sprinkled with chopped parsley and accompanied by fingers, or triangles of hot toast and a bowl of plain boiled rice.

Kidney risotto

Metric	Imperial
1 onion, peeled and finely chopped	1 onion, peeled and finely chopped
1 green pepper, cored, seeded and finely chopped	1 green pepper, cored, seeded and finely chopped
2×15 ml spoons oil	2 tablespoons oil
8 lamb's kidneys, halved, cored and chopped	8 lamb's kidneys, halved, cored and chopped
225 g long-grain rice	8 oz long-grain rice
600 ml chicken stock	1 pint chicken stock
salt	salt
freshly ground black pepper	freshly ground black pepper
50 g butter	2 oz butter
2×15 ml spoons chopped fresh parsley	2 tablespoons chopped fresh parsley
50 g grated Parmesan cheese	2 oz grated Parmesan cheese

Preparation and cooking time: 40 minutes

Fry the onion and green pepper in the oil for 2 to 3 minutes. Add the chopped kidneys and fry, stirring for a further 2 minutes. Stir in the rice and cook for 1 minute. Gradually stir in the stock, bring to the boil, then add salt and pepper to taste.
Cover the pan and simmer gently for 20 minutes until the rice has absorbed all the liquid. Stir in the butter, parsley and Parmesan cheese, and serve immediately with a tossed green salad.

Liver lyonnaise

Metric	Imperial
750 g calf's liver, thinly sliced	1½ lb calf's liver, thinly sliced
seasoned flour	seasoned flour
2 large onions, peeled and sliced	2 large onions, peeled and sliced
25 g butter	1 oz butter
1×15 ml spoon oil	1 tablespoon oil
150 ml beef stock	¼ pint beef stock
150 ml dry cider	¼ pint dry cider
salt	salt
freshly ground black pepper	freshly ground black pepper
2×15 ml spoons chopped fresh parsley	2 tablespoons chopped fresh parsley

Preparation and cooking time: 20 minutes

Dust the sliced liver in seasoned flour. Fry the sliced onions in the butter and oil for 2 to 3 minutes. Add the liver and fry until lightly browned on all sides. Gradually stir in the stock, cider, and salt and pepper. Cover and simmer gently for 10 to 12 minutes. Sprinkle with chopped parsley before serving.
Serve with mashed potato and a tomato salad.
Vegetable tip: peel the potatoes, cut into small pieces and boil them while the liver is cooking. Drain and mash the potatoes with a little butter and milk, and salt and pepper to taste.

Liver stroganoff

Metric
750 g calf's or lamb's liver,
  cut into strips, 5 mm
  thick
seasoned flour
1 medium onion, peeled and
  finely chopped
50 g butter
100 g button mushrooms,
  sliced
6×15 ml spoons dry sherry
salt
freshly ground black pepper
150 ml soured cream

Imperial
1½ lb calf's or lamb's liver,
  cut into strips, ¼ inch
  thick
seasoned flour
1 medium onion, peeled and
  finely chopped
2 oz butter
4 oz button mushrooms,
  sliced
6 tablespoons dry sherry
salt
freshly ground black pepper
¼ pint soured cream

From left: Kidney risotto; Liver lyonnaise;
Liver stroganoff

Preparation and cooking time: 25 minutes

Dust the strips of liver in seasoned flour, then shake
off any surplus flour.
Fry the onion gently in the butter for 2 minutes in a
shallow frying pan. Add the liver and continue frying,
stirring occasionally, until the liver begins to colour.
Add the mushrooms and fry for a further 3 minutes.
Add the sherry, and salt and pepper. Cover and
simmer for 5 minutes.
Stir in the soured cream and heat through carefully,
without boiling. Serve with boiled noodles and a salad.
Vegetable tip: start cooking the noodles in boiling
salted water when you add the sherry to the liver. Toss
the drained cooked noodles in butter.

COOK-AHEAD MEALS

When you are really short of time, a cook-ahead meal can be the answer. All the preparation and most of the cooking can be done the night before, when you have a little time to spare, and the dish can then be finished off on the following day, and you will have plenty of time to make a really interesting vegetable dish. Most of the cook-ahead dishes actually improve for being made in advance, so you save time and gain flavour.

Lamb and chick pea ragoût

Metric	Imperial
175 g chick peas, soaked in hot water for 4 hours	6 oz chick peas, soaked in hot water for 4 hours
2 medium onions, peeled and sliced	2 medium onions, peeled and sliced
2×15 ml spoons oil	2 tablespoons oil
1 kg middle neck of lamb	2¼ lb middle neck of lamb
2×15 ml spoons plain flour	2 tablespoons plain flour
450 ml chicken stock	¾ pint chicken stock
300 ml apple juice	½ pint apple juice
225 g carrots, peeled and thinly sliced	8 oz carrots, peeled and thinly sliced
salt	salt
freshly ground black pepper	freshly ground black pepper

Advance preparation and cooking time: 1¾ hours (excluding soaking time)
Cooking time on the day: 40 minutes
Oven: 180°C, 350°F, Gas Mark 4

Drain the chick peas and put into a pan with fresh water to cover. Bring to the boil and simmer for 30 minutes. Drain.
Meanwhile, fry the onions in the oil for 3 minutes. Add the lamb pieces and cook over moderate heat until lightly browned on all sides. Stir in the flour, then gradually add the stock and apple juice. Bring to the boil and add the carrots and salt and pepper. Cover and simmer for 1 hour. Transfer the mixture to a casserole and add the drained chick peas. Cover and chill in the refrigerator overnight.
On the day: cook in a covered casserole in a preheated oven for 40 minutes. Serve with a green salad.

Spiced Hawaiian lamb with limes

Metric	Imperial
2 onions, peeled and sliced	2 onions, peeled and sliced
3×15 ml spoons oil	3 tablespoons oil
750 g lamb fillet, cubed	1½ lb lamb fillet, cubed
pinch of ground cinnamon	pinch of ground cinnamon
pinch of ground cloves	pinch of ground cloves
2×15 ml spoons plain flour	2 tablespoons plain flour
300 ml pineapple juice	½ pint pineapple juice
300 ml chicken stock	½ pint chicken stock
3 limes or 2 lemons	3 limes or 2 lemons
sprigs of fresh mint or rosemary, to garnish	sprigs of fresh mint or rosemary, to garnish

Advance preparation and cooking time: 45 minutes
Preparation and cooking time on the day: 40 minutes
Oven: 180°C, 350°F, Gas Mark 4

Fry the onions gently in the oil for 3 minutes. Add the cubed lamb and cook over moderate heat until lightly browned on all sides. Stir in the cinnamon, cloves and the flour and cook for 1 minute. Gradually stir in the pineapple juice and chicken stock. Squeeze the juice from 2 of the limes (or 1½ lemons) and add to the pan. Cover and simmer for 30 minutes. Cool the mixture, then chill in the refrigerator overnight.
On the day: cook in the oven for 40 minutes. Serve garnished with thin slices of the remaining lime or ½ lemon, and small sprigs of mint.

Lamb and chick pea ragoût; Spiced Hawaiian lamb with limes

Simple cassoulet

Simple cassoulet

Metric
100 g dried red kidney beans
100 g dried haricot beans
2 medium onions, peeled
  and sliced
3×15 ml spoons oil
2 garlic cloves, crushed
450 g tomatoes, coarsely
  chopped
1×15 ml spoon tomato
  purée
1×15 ml spoon black treacle
300 ml beef stock
salt
freshly ground black pepper
100 g lean gammon, diced
4 chicken wings
175 g spiced smoked
  sausage, diced
50 g butter
2×15 ml spoons dried
  breadcrumbs
50 g grated cheese

Imperial
4 oz dried red kidney beans
4 oz dried haricot beans
2 medium onions, peeled
  and sliced
3 tablespoons oil
2 garlic cloves, crushed
1 lb tomatoes, coarsely
  chopped
1 tablespoon tomato
  purée
1 tablespoon black treacle
½ pint beef stock
salt
freshly ground black pepper
4 oz lean gammon, diced
4 chicken wings
6 oz spiced smoked
  sausage, diced
2 oz butter
2 tablespoons dried
  breadcrumbs
2 oz grated cheese

Advance preparation and cooking time: 1½ hours
(excluding soaking time)
Preparation and cooking time on the day: 40 minutes
Oven: 180°C, 350°F, Gas Mark 4

Soak the dried beans in cold water for 6 hours or
overnight, then drain.
Fry the onions gently in the oil for 3 minutes. Add the
garlic, tomatoes, tomato purée, treacle, stock, beans
and salt and pepper. Bring to the boil and boil for 10
minutes. Stir in the drained beans.
Fry the diced gammon, chicken wings, and the diced
smoked sausage in the butter over moderate heat until
lightly browned.
Put half the bean mixture into a casserole, add the
meats, then cover with the remaining beans. Cover the
casserole and cook in a preheated over for 1¼ hours.
Cool, then chill in the refrigerator overnight.
On the day: remove the lid from the casserole and stir
the ingredients. Sprinkle the top with the breadcrumbs and grated cheese and return to the oven,
uncovered, for 35 minutes.

Ham and rice stuffed cabbage leaves

Metric	Imperial
1 green cabbage	*1 green cabbage*
salt	*salt*
175 g long-grain rice	*6 oz long-grain rice*
25 g butter	*1 oz butter*
100 g cooked ham, finely chopped	*4 oz cooked ham, finely chopped*
50 g currants	*2 oz currants*
2×15 ml spoons chopped fresh parsley	*2 tablespoons chopped fresh parsley*
2 egg yolks	*2 egg yolks*
salt	*salt*
freshly ground black pepper	*freshly ground black pepper*
150 ml single cream	*¼ pint single cream*
paprika	*paprika*

Advance preparation and cooking time: 25 minutes
Preparation and cooking time on the day: 30 minutes
Oven: 180°C, 350°F, Gas Mark 4

This dish is made with cabbage leaves which are an excellent alternative to vine leaves, although these can be used, if preferred. However, a larger number of vine leaves may be needed, depending on their size.

Select 12 good sized leaves from the cabbage (use the small centre leaves for shredding into a salad).
Cut away the thick centre stalk from each leaf. Plunge the leaves into a pan of boiling salted water and cook for 5 minutes. Remove the cabbage leaves carefully from the pan, and drain them flat on absorbent kitchen paper.
Meanwhile, cook the rice in boiling salted water for 10 minutes and drain it thoroughly. Mix the cooked rice with the butter, ham, currants, parsley, egg yolks, and salt and pepper to taste.
Divide the rice mixture equally among the cabbage leaves, then roll each one up into a parcel, turning the edges of the leaves in. Place the stuffed cabbage leaves close together in an ovenproof dish. Cover tightly with cling film and chill in the refrigerator overnight.
On the day: spoon the cream over the stuffed cabbage leaves and sprinkle with paprika. Cook in a preheated oven for 30 minutes.

Ham and rice stuffed cabbage leaves

Stuffed courgettes with neapolitan sauce

Advance preparation and cooking time: 45 minutes
Preparation and cooking time on the day: 30 minutes
Oven: 190°C, 375°F, Gas Mark 5

Metric
8 large courgettes
1 onion, peeled and chopped
2 × 15 ml spoons oil
4 streaky bacon rashers,
    rinded and chopped
225 g minced pork
50 g fresh breadcrumbs
1 egg, beaten
3 × 15 ml spoons chopped
    fresh parsley
salt
freshly ground black pepper

Sauce:
1 onion, peeled and sliced
2 × 15 ml spoons oil
450 g tomatoes, roughly
    chopped
150 ml red wine
grated rind and juice of 1
    lemon
1 × 15 ml spoon tomato
    purée
2 × 5 ml spoons caster sugar
1 garlic clove, crushed

Imperial
8 large courgettes
1 onion, peeled and chopped
2 tablespoons oil
4 streaky bacon rashers,
    rinded and chopped
8 oz minced pork
2 oz fresh breadcrumbs
1 egg, beaten
3 tablespoons chopped fresh
    parsley
salt
freshly ground black pepper

Sauce:
1 onion, peeled and sliced
2 tablespoons oil
1 lb tomatoes, roughly
    chopped
¼ pint red wine
grated rind and juice of 1
    lemon
1 tablespoon tomato
    purée
2 teaspoons caster sugar
1 garlic clove, crushed

Trim the ends off the courgettes, then cut the courgettes in half lengthways and scoop out the centres to give boat shapes. Roughly chop the scooped out courgette flesh and set aside.

Meanwhile, fry the chopped onion in the oil for 2 minutes. Add the bacon and the minced pork and cook, stirring, until lightly browned. Add the courgette flesh and cook for a further 2 minutes. Stir in the breadcrumbs, beaten egg, chopped parsley, and salt and pepper to taste.

Fill the hollowed courgettes with the meat mixture and arrange in a greased ovenproof dish. Pour a little oil over each courgette, cover and bake in a preheated oven for 30 minutes.

Meanwhile, make the sauce. Fry the sliced onion in the oil for 2 minutes. Add the chopped tomatoes, red wine, lemon rind and juice, tomato purée, sugar, garlic, and salt and pepper. Bring to the boil, then simmer for 10 minutes. Pour the sauce over the baked courgettes. Cool, re-cover and chill in the refrigerator overnight.

On the day: cook the courgettes in a preheated oven for 30 minutes.

Stuffed courgettes with neapolitan sauce;
Braised pork in orange sauce

Braised pork in orange sauce

Metric

2 medium onions, peeled
   and chopped
3 × 15 ml spoons oil
500 g pork fillet, cubed
seasoned flour
300 ml pure orange juice
150 ml chicken stock
225 g carrots, peeled and
   grated
pinch of ground cinnamon
salt
freshly ground black pepper
2 oranges, peel and pith
   removed, cut into
   segments
150 ml double cream
2 × 15 ml spoons chopped
   walnuts

Imperial

2 medium onions, peeled
   and chopped
3 tablespoons oil
1¼ lb pork fillet, cubed
seasoned flour
½ pint pure orange juice
¼ pint chicken stock
8 oz carrots, peeled and
   grated
pinch of ground cinnamon
salt
freshly ground black pepper
2 oranges, peel and pith
   removed, cut into
   segments
¼ pint double cream
2 tablespoons chopped
   walnuts

Advance preparation and cooking time: 45 minutes
Preparation and cooking time on the day: 40 minutes
Oven: 180°C, 350°F, Gas Mark 4

Fry the chopped onion in the oil for 3 minutes over low
heat. Dust the cubed pork in seasoned flour and add to
the onion. Cook over moderate heat until the meat is
lightly browned on all sides. Gradually stir in the
orange juice and chicken stock. Bring to the boil and
add the carrot, cinnamon, and salt and pepper. Cover
and simmer gently for 30 minutes.
Stir in the orange segments, double cream and walnuts
and allow to cool. Transfer to a casserole, cover and
chill in the refrigerator overnight.
On the day: cook in a covered casserole in a preheated
oven for 40 minutes.

Cabbage and beef loaf

Advance preparation and cooking time: 1 hour
Preparation and cooking time on the day: 30 minutes
Oven: 180°C, 350°F, Gas Mark 4

Metric
8 large cabbage leaves
450 g minced beef
1 medium onion, peeled and
  grated
75 g fresh breadcrumbs
2 eggs, beaten
3 × 15 ml spoons double
  cream
1 garlic clove, crushed
1 × 15 ml spoon
  Worcestershire sauce
salt
freshly ground black pepper
1 × 15 ml spoon French
  mustard
100 g Cheddar cheese,
  grated

Imperial
8 large cabbage leaves
1 lb minced beef
1 medium onion, peeled and
  grated
3 oz fresh breadcrumbs
2 eggs, beaten
3 tablespoons double
  cream
1 garlic clove, crushed
1 tablespoon Worcestershire
  sauce
salt
freshly ground black pepper
1 tablespoon French
  mustard
4 oz Cheddar cheese,
  grated

Put the cabbage leaves into a bowl and pour over
enough boiling water to cover. Leave for 3 to 4
minutes, then drain and pat the leaves dry.
Grease a small loaf tin or soufflé dish and line it with 6
of the cabbage leaves overlapping one another.
Mix the minced beef with the onion, breadcrumbs,
beaten eggs, cream, garlic, Worcestershire sauce, and
salt and pepper. Press the mixture into the cabbage
lined dish. Cover with the remaining cabbage leaves
and a piece of greased foil. Stand the dish in a roasting
tin and pour in sufficient boiling water to come half-
way up the sides of the dish. Bake in a preheated oven
for 45 minutes.
Allow the loaf to cool in its tin, then store in the
refrigerator overnight.
On the day: unmould the loaf on to a shallow ovenproof dish. Spread the top with a thin layer of the
mustard and sprinkle with the grated cheese. Bake in
the oven for 25 minutes until the loaf is heated through
and the cheese is lightly browned.

From left: Cabbage and beef loaf; Spiced moussaka

Spiced moussaka

Metric

1 large aubergine, thinly
  sliced
3×15 ml spoons oil
1 medium onion, peeled and
  finely chopped
450 g minced beef
1×15 ml spoon paprika
1 garlic clove, crushed
2×15 ml spoons tomato
  purée
100 g mushrooms, chopped
300 ml chicken or beef stock
salt
freshly ground black pepper

Topping:
150 ml plain unsweetened
  yogurt
1 egg
75 g Cheddar cheese, grated

Imperial

1 large aubergine, thinly
  sliced
3 tablespoons oil
1 medium onion, peeled and
  finely chopped
1 lb minced beef
1 tablespoon paprika
1 garlic clove, crushed
2 tablespoons tomato
  purée
4 oz mushrooms, chopped
½ pint chicken or beef stock
salt
freshly ground black pepper

Topping:
¼ pint plain unsweetened
  yogurt
1 egg
3 oz Cheddar cheese, grated

Advance preparation and cooking time: 50 minutes
Preparation and cooking time on the day: 30 minutes
Oven: 190°C, 375°F, Gas Mark 5

Arrange the aubergine slices on lightly oiled baking
sheets, then bake in a preheated oven for 15 minutes.
Meanwhile make the meat sauce. Fry the onion in the
remaining oil for 2 minutes. Add the minced beef and
cook, stirring, until lightly browned. Stir in the paprika and cook for 1 minute. Add the garlic, tomato
purée, mushrooms, stock and salt and pepper. Cover
and simmer the sauce for 15 minutes.
Arrange the aubergine slices and meat sauce in alter-
nate layers in a greased ovenproof dish, starting with
sauce and finishing with aubergine. Brush the top
layer of aubergine slices with oil and cover the dish
with foil. Bake in the oven for 20 minutes, then allow
to cool and chill in the refrigerator overnight.
On the day: beat the yogurt with the egg and the grated
cheese and spoon the mixture over the top of the
moussaka. Bake in a preheated oven for 25 minutes.

47

Italian veal hotpot

Italian veal hotpot

Metric
4 pieces shin of veal
3×15 ml spoons oil
2 medium onions, peeled
  and finely chopped
450 g tomatoes, seeded and
  chopped
2 garlic cloves, finely
  chopped
1×15 ml spoon chopped
  fresh basil (or 1×5 ml
  spoon dried basil)
1×5 ml spoon caster sugar
300 ml dry white wine
salt
freshly ground black pepper
grated rind of 1 lemon
3×15 ml spoons chopped
  fresh parsley

·Imperial
4 pieces shin of veal
3 tablespoons oil
2 medium onions, peeled
  and finely chopped
1 lb tomatoes, seeded and
  chopped
2 garlic cloves, finely
  chopped
1 tablespoon chopped
  fresh basil (or 1 teaspoon
  dried basil)
1 teaspoon caster sugar
½ pint dry white wine
salt
freshly ground black pepper
grated rind of 1 lemon
3 tablespoons chopped
  fresh parsley

Advance preparation and cooking time: 1 hour
Preparation and cooking time on the day: 40 minutes
Oven: 180°C, 350°F, Gas Mark 4

Fry the pieces of veal in the oil until browned on all
sides, then remove them to a plate.
Add the onion to the fat remaining in the pan and fry
gently for 2 minutes. Add the tomatoes, one of the
chopped cloves of garlic, basil, sugar, wine and salt
and pepper. Bring to the boil and simmer for 5
minutes.
Return the pieces of veal to the pan, then cover and
simmer for 45 minutes. Transfer to a casserole and
cool. Cover and chill in the refrigerator overnight.
On the day: cook in a covered casserole in a preheated
oven for 40 minutes. Mix the remaining chopped
garlic with the lemon rind and parsley and sprinkle
over the veal just before serving.

Overnight pizza

Metric	Imperial
1 ×275 g packet white bread mix	1 ×10 oz packet white bread mix
oil	oil
6 tomatoes, seeded and chopped	6 tomatoes, seeded and chopped
2 ×15 ml spoons tomato purée	2 tablespoons tomato purée
1 garlic clove, crushed	1 garlic clove, crushed
4 ×15 ml spoons oil	4 tablespoons oil
75 g sliced garlic sausage	3 oz sliced garlic sausage
175 g Mozzarella cheese, sliced	6 oz Mozzarella cheese, sliced
1 ×5 ml spoon dried oregano	1 teaspoon dried oregano
salt	salt
freshly ground black pepper	freshly ground black pepper

Advance preparation and cooking time: 20 minutes
Preparation and cooking time on the day: 25 to 30 minutes
Oven: 220°C, 425°F, Gas Mark 7

Make up the bread mix according to the directions on the packet. Knead the dough for 5 minutes on a lightly floured surface. Roll out to a large circle, 25 cm/10 inches in diameter, and then place it on a greased baking sheet.

Mix the chopped tomatoes with the tomato purée, garlic and 2 ×15 ml spoons (2 tablespoons) of the oil, then spread evenly over the pizza base. Cover with overlapping slices of garlic sausage and cheese. Brush generously with oil. Sprinkle over the oregano, and salt and pepper.

Put the pizza, on the baking sheet, into a large polythene bag, making sure that there is space between the bag and the top of the pizza. Refrigerate overnight, to allow the pizza dough to rise.

On the day: remove the pizza from the bag, then sprinkle the top of the pizza generously with the remaining oil. Bake in a preheated oven for 25 to 30 minutes.

Variations

Use 100 g (4 oz) lightly fried, sliced button mushrooms in place of the garlic sausage.

Omit the garlic sausage and arrange a lattice of anchovy fillets on top of the Mozzarella cheese. Add a few black olives.

Overnight pizza

Beef and prune casserole

Metric	Imperial
100 g dried prunes	4 oz dried prunes
300 ml hot black tea, strained	½ pint hot black tea, strained
2 medium onions, peeled and sliced	2 medium onions, peeled and sliced
3 × 15 ml spoons oil	3 tablespoons oil
500 g stewing steak, cubed	1¼ lb stewing steak, cubed
4 lamb's kidneys, halved, cored and chopped	4 lamb's kidneys, halved, cored and chopped
seasoned flour	seasoned flour
600 ml beef stock	1 pint beef stock
2 × 15 ml spoons redcurrant jelly	2 tablespoons redcurrant jelly
large strip of orange peel	large strip of orange peel

Advance preparation and cooking time: 1¾ hours
Preparation and cooking time on the day: 30 minutes
Oven: 190°C, 375°F, Gas Mark 5

Cover the prunes with the hot tea and leave to stand for 30 minutes.
Fry the onions gently in the oil for 3 minutes. Dust the cubed steak and chopped kidneys in the seasoned flour and add to the onion. Fry over moderate heat until the meats are lightly browned. Gradually stir in the stock and the redcurrant jelly. Bring to the boil and simmer for 10 minutes. Add the prunes and their soaking liquid, and the orange peel. Cover and continue simmering gently for 1 hour. Allow to cool, then chill in the refrigerator overnight.
On the day: heat through in a covered casserole in a preheated oven for 30 minutes.

Egg and beef goulash

Metric	Imperial
1 medium onion, peeled and finely chopped	1 medium onion, peeled and finely chopped
4 celery sticks, finely chopped	4 celery sticks, finely chopped
450 g stewing steak, cubed	1 lb stewing steak, cubed
seasoned flour	seasoned flour
2 × 15 ml spoons paprika	2 tablespoons paprika
1 × 15 ml spoon tomato purée	1 tablespoon tomato purée
450 ml chicken stock	¾ pint chicken stock
salt	salt
150 ml soured cream	¼ pint soured cream
4 hard-boiled eggs, halved	4 hard-boiled eggs, halved

Advance preparation and cooking time: 1¼ hours
Preparation and cooking time on the day: 40 minutes
Oven: 180°C, 350°F, Gas Mark 4

Fry the onion and celery gently in the oil for 3 minutes. Dust the cubed meat in seasoned flour and add to the vegetables. Cook over moderate heat until the meat is lightly browned on all sides. Stir in the paprika and cook for 1 minute. Add the tomato purée, chicken stock, and salt. Bring to the boil and simmer for 1 hour.
Stir in the soured cream and the hard-boiled eggs, then allow to cool. Transfer to a casserole, cover and chill in the refrigerator overnight.
On the day: cook in a covered casserole in a preheated oven for 40 minutes.

Egg and beef goulash; Beef and prune casserole; Chilli beef

Chilli beef

Metric
2 medium onions, peeled
and finely chopped
2 × 15 ml spoons oil
750 g minced beef
1 × 15 ml spoon chilli
powder
300 ml beef stock
150 ml tomato juice
2 red peppers, cored, seeded
and chopped
salt
freshly ground black pepper

Imperial
2 medium onions, peeled
and finely chopped
2 tablespoons oil
1½ lb minced beef
1 tablespoon chilli
powder
½ pint beef stock
¼ pint tomato juice
2 red peppers, cored, seeded
and chopped
salt
freshly ground black pepper

Advance preparation and cooking time: 40 minutes
Preparation and cooking time on the day: 30 minutes
Oven: 180°C, 350°F, Gas Mark 4

Chilli powders vary in strength depending on the manufacturer, so it is best to use it cautiously until you find the right strength to suit your taste.

Fry the onions gently in the oil for 3 minutes. Add the mince and cook, stirring, over moderate heat until lightly browned. Stir in the chilli powder and cook for 1 minute. Add all the remaining ingredients and bring to the boil. Cover and simmer gently for 30 minutes. Transfer to a casserole and cool. Cover and chill in the refrigerator overnight.
On the day: cook in a covered casserole in a preheated oven for 30 minutes, adding a little extra liquid, either beef stock or tomato juice, if necessary.

Tuna lasagne

Metric
1 onion, peeled and chopped
25 g butter
1×15 ml spoon plain flour
300 ml chicken stock
300 ml milk
200 g can tuna, drained and
    flaked
salt
freshly ground black pepper
grated rind of ½ lemon
3 hard-boiled eggs
175 g lasagne
150 ml double cream
1 egg
2×15 ml spoons chopped
    fresh parsley

Imperial
1 onion, peeled and chopped
1 oz butter
1 tablespoon plain flour
½ pint chicken stock
½ pint milk
7 oz can tuna, drained and
    flaked
salt
freshly ground black pepper
grated rind of ½ lemon
3 hard-boiled eggs
6 oz lasagne
¼ pint double cream
1 egg
2 tablespoons chopped
    fresh parsley

Tuna lasagne; Chicken tonnato

Advance preparation and cooking time: 40 minutes
Preparation and cooking time on the day: 25 minutes
Oven: 190°C, 375°F, Gas Mark 5

Fry the onion gently in the butter for 3 minutes. Stir in the flour and cook for 1 minute. Remove the pan from the heat and gradually stir in the chicken stock and milk. Bring to the boil, stirring until lightly thickened. Add the tuna, salt and pepper to taste, the lemon rind and one of the hard-boiled eggs, chopped.
Layer the sauce and the dry sheets of lasagne in a greased ovenproof dish, starting and finishing with sauce. Bake in a preheated oven for 25 minutes, covered with a piece of greased foil. Cool and chill.
On the day: beat the cream lightly with the egg and stir in the parsley. Spoon evenly over the lasagne and thickly slice and arrange the remaining hard-boiled eggs on top. Bake in a preheated oven for 20 minutes.

Chicken tonnato

Metric
1 × 1½ kg roasting chicken
juice of 2 lemons
bay leaf
few parsley stalks
1 small onion, peeled and
    stuck with 3 cloves
salt

Sauce:
1 × 200 g can tuna
300 ml mayonnaise
2 garlic cloves, crushed
few drops of Tabasco
3 × 15 ml spoons capers
3 × 15 ml spoons chopped
    fresh parsley
2 cans anchovy fillets
freshly ground black pepper

Imperial
1 × 3 lb roasting chicken
juice of 2 lemons
bay leaf
few parsley stalks
1 small onion, peeled and
    stuck with 3 cloves
salt

Sauce:
1 × 7 oz can tuna
½ pint mayonnaise
2 garlic cloves, crushed
few drops of Tabasco
3 tablespoons capers
3 tablespoons chopped
    fresh parsley
2 cans anchovy fillets
freshly ground black pepper

Advance preparation and cooking time: 1½ hours
Preparation and cooking time on the day: 5 minutes

Put the chicken into a large pan with half the lemon juice, the bay leaf, parsley stalks, onion stuck with cloves, and 1 × 5 ml spoon/1 teaspoon salt. Add sufficient water to almost cover the chicken. Cover the pan and bring to the boil, then simmer for 1 hour.
Meanwhile make the tonnato sauce. Put the drained tuna into the liquidizer with the mayonnaise, remaining lemon juice, garlic, Tabasco, 1 × 15 ml spoon/1 tablespoon of the capers, 2 × 15 ml spoons/2 tablespoons of the parsley, 1 of the cans of drained anchovy fillets, and pepper. Blend until smooth.
Remove the cooked chicken on to a chopping board. Using a large carving fork and knife, remove all the chicken meat, while it is still hot. Arrange the pieces of chicken on a serving dish, and immediately spoon the sauce over the top. Cover loosely with foil and chill in the refrigerator overnight.
On the day: garnish with the remaining capers, chopped parsley and anchovy fillets. Serve cold.

53

Fish curry

Metric	Imperial
1 medium onion, peeled and sliced	1 medium onion, peeled and sliced
2×15 ml spoons oil	2 tablespoons oil
1 red pepper, cored, seeded and chopped	1 red pepper, cored, seeded and chopped
1×15 ml spoon curry powder	1 tablespoon curry powder
1×15 ml spoon plain flour	1 tablespoon plain flour
450 ml chicken stock	¾ pint chicken stock
50 g sultanas	2 oz sultanas
juice and grated rind of ½ lemon	juice and grated rind of ½ lemon
½ cucumber, seeded and chopped	½ cucumber, seeded and chopped
150 ml soured cream	¼ pint soured cream
4 cod cutlets	4 cod cutlets
salt	salt
freshly ground black pepper	freshly ground black pepper
2×15 ml spoons desiccated coconut, toasted	2 tablespoons desiccated coconut, toasted

Advance preparation and cooking time: 35 minutes
Preparation and cooking time on the day: 30 minutes
Oven: 180°C, 350°F, Gas Mark 4

Fry the sliced onion gently in the oil for 2 minutes. Add the red pepper and the curry powder and fry, stirring, for a further minute. Stir in the flour, then gradually add the chicken stock. Add the sultanas and the lemon juice and rind and simmer for 10 minutes. Add the chopped cucumber, soured cream, cod cutlets and salt and pepper. Simmer for a further 12 to 15 minutes. Cool, then cover and chill in the refrigerator. On the day: heat through in a shallow ovenproof dish in a preheated oven for 30 minutes. Sprinkle with the toasted coconut before serving.

Creamy chicken curry

Metric	Imperial
75 g desiccated coconut	3 oz desiccated coconut
300 ml boiling water	½ pint boiling water
2 medium onions, peeled and sliced	2 medium onions, peeled and sliced
2×15 ml spoons oil	2 tablespoons oil
1×15 ml spoon curry powder	1 tablespoon curry powder
1×15 ml spoon plain flour	1 tablespoon plain flour
1×15 ml spoon tomato purée	1 tablespoon tomato purée
300 ml chicken stock	½ pint chicken stock
2 eating apples, cored and chopped	2 eating apples, cored and chopped
50 g raisins	2 oz raisins
3×15 ml spoons double cream	3 tablespoons double cream
50 g cashew nuts	2 oz cashew nuts
salt	salt
freshly ground black pepper	freshly ground black pepper
350 g cooked chicken, chopped	12 oz cooked chicken, chopped

Advance preparation and cooking time: 40 minutes
Preparation and cooking time on the day: 40 minutes
Oven: 180°C, 350°F, Gas Mark 4

If you buy the chicken meat ready cooked, you will need about half a good sized chicken.

Put the coconut in a bowl and pour over the boiling water. Leave to stand for 30 minutes.
Meanwhile, fry the onions in the oil for 2 minutes. Stir in the curry powder and the flour and cook for 1 minute. Stir in the tomato purée and the stock and bring to the boil. Add the apples, raisins, cream, cashew nuts and salt and pepper and simmer gently for 20 minutes.
Pour the coconut and its liquid into a sieve and press the coconut to extract all the flavour. Add the coconut milk and the chopped cooked chicken to the curry sauce. Put into a casserole, cover and chill in the refrigerator overnight.
On the day: cook in a covered casserole in a preheated oven for 40 minutes.

Clockwise from top: Creamy chicken curry; Lentil curry; Fish curry

Lentil curry

Metric
225 g lentils, soaked in hot
water for 4 hours
2 onions, peeled and
sliced
100 g streaky bacon,
rinded and chopped
2×15 ml spoons oil
2×15 ml spoons curry
powder
300 ml chicken stock
300 ml milk
grated rind of ½ lemon
225 g boiling ring sausage,
sliced
salt
freshly ground black pepper
150 ml single cream
50 g salted peanuts

Imperial
8 oz lentils, soaked in hot
water for 4 hours
2 onions, peeled and
sliced
4 oz streaky bacon,
rinded and chopped
2 tablespoons oil
2 tablespoons curry
powder
½ pint chicken stock
½ pint milk
grated rind of ½ lemon
8 oz boiling ring sausage,
sliced
salt
freshly ground black pepper
¼ pint single cream
2 oz salted peanuts

Advance preparation and cooking time: 1 hour
(excluding soaking time)
Preparation and cooking time on the day: 30 minutes
Oven: 180°C, 350°F, Gas Mark 4

Drain the lentils, then put them into a pan with
enough fresh water to cover. Cover the pan and simmer for 30 minutes.
Fry the onions and chopped bacon gently in the oil for
3 minutes. Stir in the curry powder and cook for 1
minute. Add the chicken stock, milk, lemon rind,
boiling sausage, and salt and pepper. Cover and
simmer for 20 minutes.
Add the drained lentils to the curry sauce and simmer
for a further 30 minutes. Stir in the cream and peanuts
and transfer the curry to a casserole and cool. Cover
and chill in the refrigerator overnight.
On the day: cook in a covered casserole in a preheated
oven for 30 minutes.

Indian meatballs with coconut rice

Metric
750 g minced lamb
1 onion, peeled and grated
2 × 15 ml spoons ground
   almonds
1 × 5 ml spoon turmeric
2.5 ml spoon ground ginger
2 egg yolks
salt
freshly ground black pepper
oil
2 × 15 ml spoons plain flour
1 × 15 ml spoon tomato
   purée
600 ml chicken stock
2 × 15 ml spoons mango
   chutney
4 pieces preserved stem
   ginger, chopped

Coconut rice:
225 g long-grain rice
50 g desiccated coconut
good pinch of saffron
   powder

Imperial
1½ lb minced lamb
1 onion, peeled and grated
2 tablespoons ground
   almonds
1 teaspoon turmeric
½ teaspoon ground ginger
2 egg yolks
salt
freshly ground black pepper
oil
2 tablespoons plain flour
1 tablespoon tomato
   purée
1 pint chicken stock
2 tablespoons mango
   chutney
4 pieces preserved stem
   ginger, chopped

Coconut rice:
8 oz long-grain rice
2 oz desiccated coconut
good pinch of saffron
   powder

Advance preparation and cooking time: 45 minutes
Preparation and cooking time on the day: 40 minutes
Oven: 180°C, 350°F, Gas Mark 4

Mix the minced lamb with the grated onion, ground almonds, turmeric, ground ginger, egg yolks and salt and pepper. Form the mixture into small meatballs, about the size of a walnut.

Heat sufficient oil in a large shallow pan to cover the base. Add the meatballs and fry over moderate heat until lightly browned on all sides. Remove the meatballs to a plate.

Stir the flour into the fat remaining in the pan and cook for 1 minute. Remove the pan from the heat and stir in the tomato purée, chicken stock, mango chutney and stem ginger. Bring to the boil, then return the meatballs to the pan. Cover and simmer for 25 to 30 minutes. Cool, then chill in the refrigerator.

Meanwhile, fry the rice in 2 × 15 ml spoons (2 tablespoons) oil for 2 minutes, stirring continuously. Add the dessicated coconut, saffron and 600 ml (1 pint) water. Cover and simmer gently until the rice is just tender. Drain thoroughly. Stir 4 × 15 ml spoons (4 tablespoons) oil into the rice and store overnight in the refrigerator in a covered container.

On the day: heat the meatballs in their sauce, and heat the rice through in the oven for 40 minutes.

Indian meatballs with coconut rice; Pork vindaloo-style

Pork vindaloo-style

Metric
1 × 15 ml spoon coriander
  seeds
1 × 15 ml spoon cumin seeds
1 × 15 ml spoon sesame seeds
4 cloves
3 × 15 ml spoons oil
750 g pork fillet, cubed
1 × 15 ml spoon turmeric
2 × 15 ml spoons soft brown
  sugar
150 ml wine vinegar
150 ml chicken stock or
  water
salt
freshly ground black pepper

To serve:
chopped onion
chopped green pepper
wedges of tomato
plain unsweetened yogurt
rice

Imperial
1 tablespoon coriander
  seeds
1 tablespoon cumin seeds
1 tablespoon sesame seeds
4 cloves
3 tablespoons oil
1½ lb pork fillet, cubed
1 tablespoon turmeric
2 tablespoons soft brown
  sugar
¼ pint wine vinegar
¼ pint chicken stock or
  water
salt
freshly ground black pepper

To serve:
chopped onion
chopped green pepper
wedges of tomato
plain unsweetened yogurt
rice

Advance preparation and cooking time: 1 hour
Preparation and cooking time on the day: 40 minutes
Oven: 180°C, 350°F, Gas Mark 4

Fry the coriander seeds, cumin seeds, sesame seeds and cloves in the oil for 2 minutes. Add the cubed pork fillet and fry over moderate heat until lightly browned on all sides. Add the turmeric and cook for 1 minute. Stir in the brown sugar, vinegar, stock or water, and salt and pepper. Cover and simmer very gently for 45 minutes.

There should not be very much juice with this dish, but if it becomes too dry during cooking add a little extra stock or water. Transfer to a casserole and cool. Cover and chill in the refrigerator overnight.

On the day: cook in a covered casserole in a preheated oven for 40 minutes. Transfer to a flat serving dish, and serve with small dishes of chopped onion, chopped green pepper, wedges of tomato, cooked rice and a bowl of chilled yogurt.

DESSERTS

Quick puddings usually conjure up the idea of
ice cream with canned fruit, or an instant
pudding mix. There is, however, a wide variety
of desserts that can be made in under 30
minutes – far less time than is needed for some
of the traditional favourites, such as apple pie or
trifle. Something like Lemon Zabaglione can
actually be prepared while the rest of the family
are clearing the table after the main course.

Lemon zabaglione

Metric
6 egg yolks
4×15 ml spoons caster sugar
finely grated rind of 2
 lemons
6×15 ml spoons sweet
 sherry or Marsala

Imperial
6 egg yolks
4 tablespoons caster sugar
finely grated rind of 2
 lemons
6 tablespoons sweet
 sherry or Marsala

Preparation and cooking time: 10 to 15 minutes

Put all the ingredients into a large heatproof bowl. Stand the bowl over a saucepan of gently simmering water and whisk the mixture until foamy. Take care not to let the egg mixture boil, or it will curdle. Pour into stemmed glasses and serve immediately with small sponge fingers or macaroons.

Shortcut rum babas

Metric
4 individual sponge flan
 cases
150 ml water
100 g granulated sugar
3×15 ml spoons rum
100 g seedless raisins
4×15 ml spoons apricot
 jam, warmed
200 ml double or whipping
 cream, whipped
2×15 ml spoons flaked
 almonds, toasted
4 maraschino or glacé
 cherries (optional)

Imperial
4 individual sponge flan
 cases
¼ pint water
4 oz granulated sugar
3 tablespoons rum
4 oz seedless raisins
4 tablespoons apricot
 jam, warmed
⅓ pint double or whipping
 cream, whipped
2 tablespoons flaked
 almonds, toasted
4 maraschino or glacé
 cherries (optional)

Preparation and cooking time: 30 minutes

Pierce the flan cases all over with a cocktail stick. Put the water and sugar into a pan and stir over a gentle heat until dissolved. Bring to the boil and simmer, without stirring, for 5 minutes. Stir in the rum. Dip each sponge flan case into the rum syrup until well moistened, then stand the sponges on a wire rack and brush them all over with the apricot jam. Scatter a few raisins in the bottom of each sponge case and put into the refrigerator for 5 to 10 minutes to cool. Decorate the centre of each baba with a whirl of cream, then top with a maraschino or glacé cherry, if liked and a sprinkling of toasted nuts.

Lemon zabaglione; Shortcut rum babas

Melon in ginger wine

Metric	Imperial
1 small ripe honeydew melon	1 small ripe honeydew melon
3 × 15 ml spoons ginger wine	3 tablespoons ginger wine
juice and grated rind of 1 lemon	juice and grated rind of 1 lemon
3 × 15 ml spoons caster sugar	3 tablespoons caster sugar
4 pieces preserved stem ginger, finely chopped	4 pieces preserved stem ginger, finely chopped

Preparation and cooking time: 20 minutes

This is a very refreshing dessert and is best eaten without cream.

Peel, halve, seed and cube the melon.
Mix the ginger wine with the lemon juice and rind and the sugar. Spoon the melon and its juice into individual serving dishes, pour over the ginger wine mixture and sprinkle with chopped stem ginger.

Coffee viennoise

Metric
150 ml strong black coffee
75 g soft brown sugar
100 g plain chocolate
8 scoops vanilla ice cream
4 × 15 ml spoons Tia Maria
 (optional)

Imperial
¼ pint strong black coffee
3 oz soft brown sugar
4 oz plain chocolate
8 scoops vanilla ice cream
4 tablespoons Tia Maria
 (optional)

Preparation and cooking time: 15 minutes

Use a firm ice cream, not the soft-scoop type.

Put the coffee, brown sugar and broken pieces of chocolate into a pan, then stir over a gentle heat until the sugar and chocolate have dissolved.
Put the scoops of ice cream into 4 individual dishes and spoon over the Tia Maria, if using. Top each portion with the hot coffee and chocolate sauce and serve immediately.

Cassata cheese

Metric
225 g full fat soft cheese
75 g caster sugar
grated rind of 1 orange
grated rind of 1 lemon
200 ml double cream,
 whipped
75 g almonds, toasted and
 chopped
50 g glacé cherries, chopped
75 g glacé pineapple,
 chopped

Imperial
8 oz full fat soft cheese
3 oz caster sugar
grated rind of 1 orange
grated rind of 1 lemon
⅓ pint double cream,
 whipped
3 oz almonds, toasted and
 chopped
2 oz glacé cherries, chopped
3 oz glacé pineapple,
 chopped

Preparation and cooking time: 15 minutes (excluding chilling time)

Canned pineapple, drained and chopped, may be used in place of the glacé pineapple.

Beat the cheese with the caster sugar and grated fruit rinds. Fold in the whipped cream, nuts and glacé fruits. Spoon the mixture into 4 small pots or cocotte dishes and chill for 2 to 3 hours.
Serve with boudoir sponge fingers.

From left: Melon in ginger wine;
Coffee viennoise; Cassata cheese

Paradise peach fool with almonds

Metric
3 large fresh peaches, or
 1×425 g can peaches,
 drained
juice of 1 orange
2×15 ml spoons ground
 almonds
200 ml double cream,
 chilled and whipped
2 egg whites

Imperial
3 large fresh peaches, or
 1×15 oz can peaches,
 drained
juice of 1 orange
2 tablespoons ground
 almonds
⅓ pint double cream,
 chilled and whipped
2 egg whites

Preparation and cooking time: 20 minutes

If using fresh peaches, put them in a bowl, pour over enough boiling water to cover, then leave for 1 minute. Remove the peaches with a slotted spoon to a bowl of cold water, then peel off the skins. Halve each peach and remove the stone.

Put the peaches into a liquidizer with the orange juice and blend until smooth (if the peaches are very ripe they can simply be sieved). Beat in the ground almonds and the double cream. Whisk the egg whites stiffly, then gently fold into the peach mixture with a metal spoon.

Spoon the mixture into tall glasses and serve with small macaroons or shortbread fingers.

Stuffed baked peaches

Metric
4 large ripe peaches (or 8
 large canned peach
 halves)
6×15 ml spoons stale cake
 or biscuit crumbs
few drops of almond essence
1×15 ml spoon brandy
6×15 ml spoons apricot jam
50 g flaked almonds
cream, to serve

Imperial
4 large ripe peaches (or 8
 large canned peach
 halves)
6 tablespoons stale cake
 or biscuit crumbs
few drops of almond essence
1 tablespoon brandy
6 tablespoons apricot jam
2 oz flaked almonds
cream, to serve

Preparation and cooking time: 30 minutes
Oven: 190°C, 375°F, Gas Mark 5

If using fresh peaches, put them in a bowl, pour over enough boiling water to cover, then leave for 1 minute. Remove the peaches with a slotted spoon to a bowl of cold water, then peel off the skins. Halve each peach and remove the stone.

Mix the crumbs with the almond essence, brandy and 2×15 ml spoons/2 tablespoons of the jam. Sandwich the peach halves together with the crumb mixture. Stand the peaches in an ovenproof dish, lightly greased with butter. Spoon over the remaining apricot jam and sprinkle with the flaked almonds, then bake in a preheated oven for 15 minutes. Serve the peaches hot with cream.

Stuffed baked peaches; Paradise peach fool with almonds

Raisin fritters; Sugared eggs brûlée

Sugared eggs brûlée

Metric
3 eggs
50 g caster sugar
few drops of vanilla essence
300 ml milk
4×15 ml spoons demerara
   sugar

Imperial
3 eggs
2 oz caster sugar
few drops of vanilla essence
½ pint milk
4 tablespoons demerara
   sugar

Preparation and cooking time: 30 minutes

Beat the eggs with the sugar and a few drops of vanilla essence. Warm the milk, then stir it into the beaten eggs and sugar. Pour the mixture into 4 individual ovenproof dishes. Stand the dishes in a frying pan containing 2.5 cm/1 inch of boiling water. Cover the pan and simmer the custards for 20 minutes.
Scatter the demerara sugar over the top of each custard and brown under a preheated hot grill. Serve immediately, but be careful as the sugar topping is very hot!

Raisin fritters

Metric
50 g plain flour
25 g ground almonds or
   ground rice
pinch of mixed spice
2 eggs
6×15 ml spoons double
   cream
100 g raisins
50 g caster sugar
25 g butter
2×15 ml spoons oil

Imperial
2 oz plain flour
1 oz ground almonds or
   ground rice
pinch of mixed spice
2 eggs
6 tablespoons double
   cream
4 oz raisins
2 oz caster sugar
1 oz butter
2 tablespoons oil

Sauce:
4×15 ml spoons apricot jam
juice of 2 oranges
1×15 ml spoon rum
   (optional)

Sauce:
4 tablespoons apricot jam
juice of 2 oranges
1 tablespoon rum
   (optional)

Preparation and cooking time: 20 minutes

Make the fritter batter in advance, cover and store it in the refrigerator until it is required. Then simply stir it and fry the fritters.

Put the flour, ground almonds or rice and mixed spice into a bowl. Add the eggs and the cream and beat until smooth. Stir in the raisins and the caster sugar.
Heat the butter and oil in a large shallow pan. Drop tablespoonfuls of the raisin batter into the hot fat and fry for 2 minutes. Turn the fritters and fry for a further 2 minutes. Keep the fritters warm, while frying the remaining batter. Meanwhile, put the sauce ingredients into a small pan and heat through. Serve the hot raisin fritters with the sauce.

Poor knights

Metric
8 thin slices white bread
100 g full fat soft cheese
4×15 ml spoons sultanas
4×15 ml spoons demerara
  sugar
2 eggs
4×15 ml spoons single
  cream
75 g butter

Imperial
8 thin slices white bread
4 oz full fat soft cheese
4 tablespoons sultanas
4 tablespoons demerara
  sugar
2 eggs
4 tablespoons single
  cream
3 oz butter

Preparation and cooking time: 30 minutes

Spread each slice of bread on one side with the cheese. Sprinkle half the slices of bread with sultanas and demerara sugar. Cover with the remaining four slices of bread, cheese side downwards. Press firmly together. Remove the crusts and cut each sandwich in half, either diagonally or crosswise.
Beat the eggs with the cream in a shallow bowl.
Heat the butter in a large shallow pan until bubbling. Dip each sandwich into the beaten egg and cream, until moistened on all sides, then place in the hot butter. Fry gently on both sides until crisp and golden, allowing 3 to 4 minutes for each side. Remove the sandwiches from the pan and serve immediately.
If liked, serve the poor knights with a jam sauce; heat 6×15 ml spoons/6 tablespoons jam in a small pan with 2×15 ml spoons/2 tablespoons water, while the poor knights are cooking.

Puff paste churros

Metric
225 g packet puff pastry,
  thawed
oil or fat for deep frying

Imperial
8 oz packet puff pastry,
  thawed
oil or fat for deep frying

To serve:
caster sugar
strawberries or raspberries
whipped cream

To serve:
caster sugar
strawberries or raspberries
whipped cream

Preparation and cooking time: 20 to 25 minutes

Roll out the puff pastry to 5 mm/¼ inch thickness. Cut into strips 15 cm×5 mm/6×¼ inch. If liked, tie each strip into a loose knot. Lower the pastry into a pan of hot fat or oil and deep fry until crisp and golden, about 6 minutes. Drain well on absorbent paper and dust the churros with caster sugar.
Serve while still warm with a bowl of raspberries or strawberries, when in season, and whipped cream.

Variation:
Instead of serving a seasonal berry fruit with the churros, serve a purée of cooked fruit such as apple.

Marmalade soufflé omelette

Metric	Imperial
6 eggs, separated	*6 eggs, separated*
100 g icing sugar, sifted	*4 oz icing sugar, sifted*
25 g butter	*1 oz butter*
4×15 ml spoons marmalade	*4 tablespoons marmalade*

From left: Poor knights; Puff paste churros;
Marmalade soufflé omelette

Preparation and cooking time: 20 minutes

Put the marmalade in a small pan, cover and heat through gently.
Beat the egg yolks in a bowl with half the icing sugar. Beat the egg whites stiffly and fold into the egg yolks. Heat the butter in a large shallow frying pan. Spread half the egg mixture over the pan and cook over a gentle heat until set on the underside. Put the pan under a preheated moderately hot grill until the mixture starts to rise. Spoon the warm marmalade over the partly cooked omelette, then spread the remaining egg mixture over the top. Return the pan to the grill until the omelette rises.
Sprinkle the omelette with the remaining icing sugar and brown quickly under the grill for a few seconds. Serve immediately, cut into wedges.

Menu for 6
Cold eggs Lyonnaise
"
Trout Véronique
Glazed courgettes
Potato cake
"
Chestnut Mousse

ENTERTAIN WITH EASE

Many people are put off entertaining because of the time that is involved. With a little advance planning and preparation, it is possible to entertain 6 people in a relaxed manner, without having to spend more than an hour in the kitchen on the actual day. In this section there are menus that are planned for 6 people, and two special 'panic' menus that show just how to cope when you have planned for 4 guests and 6 people turn up!

Preparation the day before:
Make the Cold Eggs Lyonnaise.
Prepare the trout, skin the grapes, cover and chill.
Slice the courgettes ready for cooking.
Cook the potatoes until tender, then drain and mash them. Mix with butter and egg yolks, shape into a large round cake on a greased baking sheet and chill.
Make the Chestnut Mousse.

One hour before dinner:
Baste, cover and start cooking the trout.
Fry the courgettes in butter and a squeeze of lemon.
Brush the potato cake with melted butter and cook in the oven until golden. Keep the vegetables warm.

Cold eggs lyonnaise

Metric	Imperial
6 hard-boiled eggs, halved	6 hard-boiled eggs, halved
450 ml consommé, chilled	¾ pint consommé, chilled
1 medium onion, peeled and roughly chopped	1 medium onion, peeled and roughly chopped
6×15 ml spoons mayonnaise	6 tablespoons mayonnaise
salt	salt
freshly ground black pepper	freshly ground black pepper

Put the hard-boiled eggs into 6 individual dishes, allowing 2 halves per person. Put the consommé into the liquidizer with the onion, mayonnaise, and salt and pepper. Blend until smooth. Spoon this mixture over the eggs, then chill until set.

Trout Véronique

Metric
6 large rainbow trout,
    cleaned
1 lemon, thinly sliced
300 ml dry white wine
salt
freshly ground black pepper
300 ml single cream
3 egg yolks
225 g green grapes, skinned
3 × 15 ml spoons chopped
    fresh parsley

Imperial
6 large rainbow trout,
    cleaned
1 lemon, thinly sliced
½ pint dry white wine
salt
freshly ground black pepper
½ pint single cream
3 egg yolks
8 oz green grapes, skinned
3 tablespoons chopped
    fresh parsley

Oven: 190°C, 375°F, Gas Mark 5

Make diagonal slits in each trout at 2.5 cm/1 inch intervals, and ease a slice of lemon into each slit. Arrange the fish in a shallow ovenproof dish, pour over the white wine, and add salt and pepper. Cover the dish and chill overnight.
Baste the fish with the marinating liquid, then cover with a piece of greased foil. Cook in a preheated oven for 30 minutes.
Remove the trout to a serving dish and keep warm. Pour the cooking liquid into a pan. Blend the cream and egg yolks together and add to the pan. Heat through over a gentle heat, stirring, until the sauce has thickened. Add the grapes, spoon the sauce over the trout and garnish with chopped parsley.

Chestnut mousse

Metric
450 ml can unsweetened
    chestnut purée
100 g soft brown sugar
finely grated rind of ½
    orange
450 ml double cream,
    whipped
2 egg whites

Imperial
¾ pint can unsweetened
    chestnut purée
4 oz soft brown sugar
finely grated rind of ½
    orange
¾ pint double cream,
    whipped
2 egg whites

Mix the chestnut purée with the brown sugar and the orange rind, then fold in the whipped cream.
Beat the egg whites until stiff, then fold into the chestnut mixture. Spoon into 6 small dishes. Chill for several hours or overnight.
The mousse may be decorated with extra whipped cream, and marrons glacé on very special occasions.

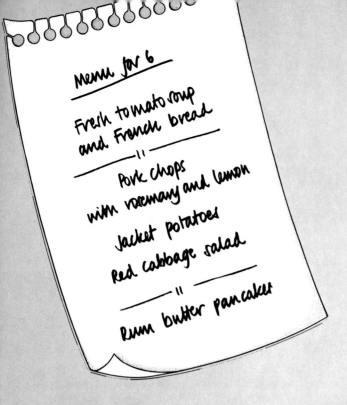

Menu for 6

*Fresh tomato soup
and French bread*

—"—

*Pork chops
with rosemary and lemon
Jacket potatoes
Red cabbage salad*

—"—

Rum butter pancakes

Fresh tomato soup

Metric	*Imperial*
750 g tomatoes	*1½ lb tomatoes*
1 medium onion, peeled and finely chopped	*1 medium onion, peeled and finely chopped*
600 ml chicken stock	*1 pint chicken stock*
150 ml red wine	*¼ pint red wine*
1×15 ml spoon wine vinegar	*1 tablespoon wine vinegar*
1×15 ml spoon sugar	*1 tablespoon sugar*
salt	*salt*
freshly ground black pepper	*freshly ground black pepper*
200 ml double cream	*⅓ pint double cream*
2 egg yolks	*2 egg yolks*

Chop the tomatoes roughly and put them into a pan with the onion, stock, red wine, vinegar, sugar, and salt and pepper to taste. Simmer the ingredients gently for 20 minutes. Blend the mixture in the liquidizer until smooth. Sieve to remove skin, if liked.
Return the soup to the pan and bring to the boil. Blend the cream with the egg yolks and add to the soup. Stir over a gentle heat until the soup thickens. Serve with hot crusty bread.

Preparation the day before:
Make the soup.
Make a red cabbage salad, with cabbage, sliced onions, sultanas and vinaigrette.
Make the pancakes and store overnight in the refrigerator, overwrapped and separated with sheets of greased greaseproof paper.
Make the rum butter.

One hour before dinner:
Bake small potatoes so that they cook more quickly, and allow 2 per person. Bake each one on a metal skewer in a preheated oven at 200°C, 400°F, Gas Mark 6.
Prepare the chops for cooking. Put them into the oven approximately 30 minutes before you serve the starter.
Spread the pancakes out on greased baking sheets and brush with melted butter. When you turn the oven off after cooking the main course, put the pancakes in to warm through in the residual heat.
Heat the soup through. Wrap a French loaf in foil and put into the oven for 3 to 4 minutes to warm.

Pork chops with rosemary and lemon

Metric
6 lean pork chops
75 g butter
garlic salt
freshly ground black pepper
2×15 ml spoons fresh
  rosemary, or 1×15 ml
  spoon dried rosemary
juice of 1 lemon

Imperial
6 lean pork chops
3 oz butter
garlic salt
freshly ground black pepper
2 tablespoons fresh
  rosemary, or 1 tablespoon
  dried rosemary
juice of 1 lemon

Oven: 200°C, 400°F, Gas Mark 6

Put the chops into a shallow ovenproof dish. Top with knobs of the butter and add garlic salt and pepper. Sprinkle with the rosemary and squeeze the lemon juice over the chops. Cover the dish with foil and cook in a preheated oven for 30 minutes.

Remove the foil and return the dish to the oven for a further 5 to 10 minutes, until the chops are tender. Serve garnished with extra sprigs of fresh rosemary and strips of lemon peel, if liked.

Rum butter pancakes

Metric
175 g butter
100 g icing sugar, sifted
3×15 ml spoons dark rum
225 g plain flour
1×2.5 ml spoon salt
2 eggs
450 ml milk
150 ml fresh orange juice
oil for frying
soft brown sugar

Imperial
6 oz butter
4 oz icing sugar, sifted
3 tablespoons dark rum
8 oz plain flour
½ teaspoon salt
2 eggs
¾ pint milk
¼ pint fresh orange juice
oil for frying
soft brown sugar

Soften the butter and beat in the sifted icing sugar and the dark rum. Put into a covered container and chill until needed.

Sift the flour and salt into a bowl. Make a well in the centre, drop in the eggs and beat them into the flour with a little of the milk to give a thick, smooth cream. Gradually whisk in the remaining milk and the orange juice. Leave the batter to stand, covered, in a cool place for 1 hour.

To cook the pancakes, heat a very little oil in a pancake or omelette pan. Add just enough batter to cover the base of the pan. Cook until lightly golden and set on the underside. Flip the pancake over and cook on the other side.

Using a lightly greased pan each time, continue with the remaining batter until you have about 12 pancakes. Keep the cooked pancakes warm between 2 clean tea towels as you cook them.

Put a spoonful of chilled rum butter on to each pancake and fold into triangles. Arrange on a serving platter, scatter over the brown sugar, and serve immediately.

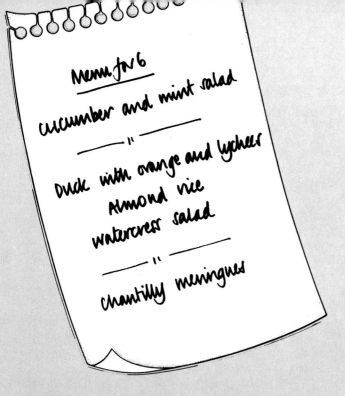

Menu for 6

cucumber and mint salad
—"—
Duck with orange and lychees
Almond rice
watercress salad
—"—
Chantilly meringues

Cucumber and mint salad

Metric	Imperial
½ large cucumber	½ large cucumber
salt	salt
grated rind and juice of 1 lemon	grated rind and juice of 1 lemon
1 garlic clove, crushed	1 garlic clove, crushed
2×5 ml spoons caster sugar	2 teaspoons caster sugar
6×15 ml spoons olive oil	6 tablespoons olive oil
freshly ground black pepper	freshly ground black pepper
4 spring onions, chopped	4 spring onions, chopped
2×15 ml spoons chopped fresh mint	2 tablespoons chopped fresh mint
few fresh mint leaves	few fresh mint leaves
pitta bread	pitta bread

Preparation the day before:
Marinate the duck.
Make the meringues.
Make vinaigrette and mint dressings for the salads.

One hour before dinner:
Start cooking the duck.
Cook the almond rice: fry 1 chopped onion and 50 g/2 oz chopped almonds in a little oil, add 175 g/6 oz rice and cook for 1 to 2 minutes. Stir in 450 ml/¾ pint chicken stock and cook until the rice is tender and the liquid absorbed. Keep warm in a serving dish.
Prepare the cucumber, drain and make the Cucumber and Mint Salad.
Toss a watercress salad in vinaigrette dressing.
Fill the meringues with chantilly cream.
Heat the pitta bread in the oven for 5 minutes.

Leave the cucumber unpeeled, and dice it. Sprinkle generously with salt and leave to drain for 20 minutes. Meanwhile, mix the lemon rind and juice with the garlic, sugar, oil, pepper, spring onions and chopped mint. Divide the drained cucumber among four shallow dishes. Spoon the mint and lemon dressing over the cucumber and decorate with mint leaves. Serve with hot pitta bread.

Duck with orange and lychees

Metric
3 small wild ducks, halved
grated rind and juice of 2
    oranges
300 g can of lychees
salt
freshly ground black pepper
100 g butter
300 ml chicken stock
1 × 15 ml spoon cornflour
2 × 15 ml spoons coarse-cut
    marmalade
watercress, to garnish

Imperial
3 small wild ducks, halved
grated rind and juice of 2
    oranges
11 oz can of lychees
salt
freshly ground black pepper
4 oz butter
½ pint chicken stock
1 tablespoon cornflour
2 tablespoons coarse-cut
    marmalade
watercress, to garnish

Oven: 200°C, 400°F, Gas Mark 6

Duckling reared for the table can be used in place of the wild ducks, if you choose small ones. Use half the butter only and cook the ducks on a rack, don't use the pan juices for the sauce as they are too greasy.

Pierce the halved ducks 4 or 5 times with a skewer. Stand them in a shallow dish and pour over the orange rind and juice, the juice from the canned lychees, and salt and pepper. Cover with cling wrap and chill overnight in the refrigerator.
Drain the duck from the marinade and put into a shallow ovenproof dish. Top the duck pieces with knobs of butter. Roast in a preheated oven for 45 minutes, basting frequently.
Meanwhile blend the chicken stock with the cornflour. Add the marinade and the marmalade, then pour into a pan ready for the sauce.
When the duck is cooked, put it on to a serving dish and keep warm. Heat the sauce ingredients in the pan, stirring until thickened, and add the sediment from the roasting pan. Add the drained lychees to the sauce and heat through. Spoon the sauce over the duck, garnish with watercress and serve.

Chantilly meringues

Metric
4 egg whites
225 g caster sugar
600 ml double cream,
    whipped
2 × 15 ml spoons coffee
    liqueur
chocolate vermicelli
few drops of coffee essence
    (optional)

Imperial
4 egg whites
8 oz caster sugar
1 pint double cream,
    whipped
2 tablespoons coffee
    liqueur
chocolate vermicelli
few drops of coffee essence
    (optional)

Oven: 120°C, 250°F, Gas Mark ½

Beat the egg whites until they form stiff peaks. Add half the caster sugar and continue beating until the meringue mixture is stiff again. Fold in the remaining caster sugar.
Using two spoons for shaping, mould the meringue into 12 mounds on greased and floured baking sheets. Cook in a preheated oven for 1½ hours. If the meringues begin to colour, turn the oven off but leave the meringues in. Cool the meringues on the baking sheets, then store them in an airtight tin.
To serve: stir the coffee liqueur into the whipped cream and colour with coffee essence, if using. Top each half meringue with the flavoured cream and sprinkle with the chocolate vermicelli.

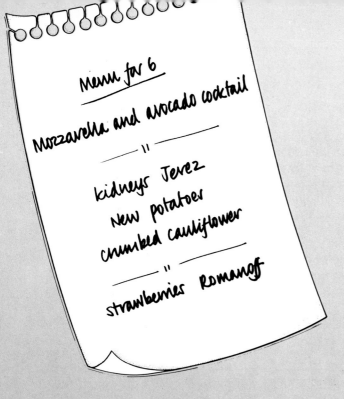

Menu for 6

Mozzarella and avocado cocktail

"

kidneys Jerez
New potatoes
crumbed cauliflower

"

strawberries Romanoff

Mozzarella and avocado cocktail

Metric	**Imperial**
150 ml olive oil	*¼ pint olive oil*
3 ×15 ml spoons wine vinegar	*3 tablespoons wine vinegar*
1 garlic clove, crushed	*1 garlic clove, crushed*
1 ×5 ml spoon French mustard	*1 teaspoon French mustard*
1 ×15 ml spoon chopped fresh basil, or 1 ×5 ml spoon dried basil	*1 tablespoon chopped fresh basil, or 1 teaspoon dried basil*
salt	*salt*
freshly ground black pepper	*freshly ground black pepper*
2 fresh Mozzarella cheeses	*2 fresh Mozzarella cheeses*
1 large ripe avocado	*1 large ripe avocado*

Mix the olive oil with the vinegar, garlic, mustard, basil, and salt and pepper to taste. Slice the Mozzarella cheeses quite thinly and put into a large shallow ovenproof dish Spoon the dressing evenly over the cheese. Cover with cling wrap and chill overnight. Peel, halve and stone the avocado. Cut the avocado into thin slices. Arrange overlapping slices of avocado and Mozzarella on individual plates, and spoon over the dressing. (Make sure that the avocado is well covered with dressing, to prevent discoloration.) Serve with thinly sliced brown bread and butter.

Preparation the day before:
Marinate the Mozzarella cheese in the dressing, ready for the cocktail.
Cook the Kidneys Jerez, cover and chill overnight in the refrigerator – they then just require reheating.
Prepare the potatoes and cauliflower for cooking.

One hour before dinner:
Make up the Strawberries Romanoff and chill.
Finish the Mozzarella and Avocado Cocktail.
Put the potatoes and cauliflower on to cook – remember that they will only take about 20 minutes.
Put the Kidneys Jerez into a casserole and heat through in a preheated oven at 180°C, 350°F, Gas Mark 4.
Put the drained cooked potatoes into a serving dish with a generous knob of butter and some chopped fresh mint. Keep warm.
Drain the cauliflower and put into a serving dish. Top with fresh breadcrumbs, fried until golden in butter. Keep warm.

Kidneys Jerez

Metric
12 large lamb's kidneys
1 medium onion, peeled and
  finely chopped
2×15 ml spoons oil
50 g butter
seasoned flour
450 ml chicken stock
150 ml medium sherry
225 g button mushrooms,
  sliced
salt
freshly ground black pepper
150 ml double cream
4×15 ml spoons coarsely
  chopped fresh parsley

Imperial
12 large lamb's kidneys
1 medium onion, peeled and
  finely chopped
2 tablespoons oil
2 oz butter
seasoned flour
¾ pint chicken stock
¼ pint medium sherry
8 oz button mushrooms,
  sliced
salt
freshly ground black pepper
¼ pint double cream
4 tablespoons coarsely
  chopped fresh parsley

If large kidneys are unobtainable, then allow 3 small ones per person.

Skin the kidneys, remove the white core, and cut into slices. Fry the chopped onion gently in the oil for 3 minutes. Dust the sliced kidneys in seasoned flour and add to the onion in the pan. Fry for 2 to 3 minutes until lightly coloured. Stir in the stock and sherry and bring to the boil. Add the mushrooms, and salt and pepper, then cover and simmer gently for 20 minutes.
Stir in the double cream and heat through carefully without boiling. Transfer the kidneys to a shallow serving dish and sprinkle over the chopped parsley. This dish reheats very well.

Strawberries Romanoff

Metric
450 g strawberries, hulled
300 ml double cream
finely grated rind of 1
  orange
2 egg whites
100 g caster sugar
3×15 ml spoons brandy
75 g ratafias, coarsely
  crushed
crystallized angelica leaves,
  to decorate

Imperial
1 lb strawberries, hulled
½ pint double cream
finely grated rind of 1
  orange
2 egg whites
4 oz caster sugar
3 tablespoons brandy
3 oz ratafias, coarsely
  crushed
crystallized angelica leaves,
  to decorate

Cut the strawberries in half. Whip the cream with the orange rind until it is thick. Beat the egg whites until stiff, then add the sugar and continue beating until the mixture holds in stiff peaks. Fold the beaten egg whites lightly into the cream, with the brandy.
Stir all but 2 of the strawberries and all the ratafias into the lightened cream. Spoon into sundae glasses and decorate with large angelica leaves and the remaining strawberries.

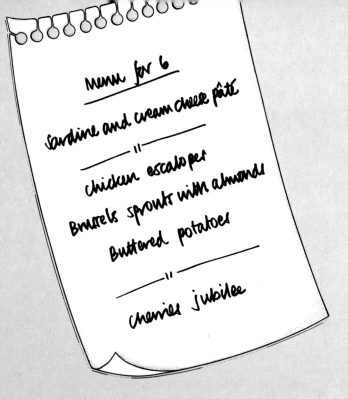

menu for 6

sardine and cream cheese pâté
"
chicken escaloper
Brussels sprouts with almonds
Buttered potatoes
"
cherries jubilee

Sardine and cream cheese pâté

Metric	Imperial
2 ×200 g can sardines, drained	2 ×7 oz can sardines, drained
grated rind and juice of ½ lemon	grated rind and juice of ½ lemon
175 g full fat soft cheese	6 oz full fat soft cheese
4 ×15 ml spoons double cream, lightly whipped	4 tablespoons double cream, lightly whipped
salt	salt
freshly ground black pepper	freshly ground black pepper

To garnish:	To garnish:
thin slices of lemon	thin slices of lemon
sprigs of fresh parsley	sprigs of fresh parsley

Mash the drained sardines, then mix with the lemon rind and juice, cheese, whipped cream, and salt and pepper to taste. Spoon the pâté into 6 small cocotte dishes, and ruffle the surface with a fork. Cover each dish with cling wrap and chill for at least 4 hours, preferably overnight.
Garnish the pâté with lemon slices and parsley and serve with fingers of hot toast.

Preparation the day before:
Make the pâté.
Flatten the escalopes and coat in breadcrumbs.
Prepare the Brussels sprouts and potatoes.
Make the garlic butter to serve with the escalopes.

One hour before dinner:
Put the pâté out – to serve it at room temperature.
Make the sauce for the Cherries Jubilee up to adding the brandy.
Put the potatoes and Brussels sprouts on to cook – remember that they will only take about 20 minutes.
Start frying the Chicken Escalopes.
Toss the cooked potatoes in butter over a gentle heat and transfer to a serving dish. Keep warm.
Fry the split almonds in the butter remaining from the potatoes. Toss together with the cooked Brussels sprouts, and put into a serving dish and keep warm.
Put the cooked escalopes on to a serving dish, cover and keep warm.
Make toast for the pâté.

Chicken escalopes

Metric
6 chicken breasts, boned and
    skinned
seasoned flour
2 eggs, beaten
fine dried breadcrumbs
225 g butter
3 × 15 ml spoons chopped
    fresh parsley
2 garlic cloves, crushed
salt
freshly ground black pepper
4 × 15 ml spoons oil

Imperial
6 chicken breasts, boned and
    skinned
seasoned flour
2 eggs, beaten
fine dried breadcrumbs
8 oz butter
3 tablespoons chopped
    fresh parsley
2 garlic cloves, crushed
salt
freshly ground black pepper
4 tablespoons oil

Flatten the chicken breasts with a meat mallet or rolling pin. Dust the flattened chicken breasts with seasoned flour, then dip them into beaten egg, and coat evenly on both sides with breadcrumbs. Place on a sheet of lightly greased greaseproof paper and chill for several hours, or overnight.

Meanwhile, soften 175 g/6 oz of the butter and mix with the chopped parsley, garlic, and salt and pepper. Place the butter mixture on a small square of grease-proof paper and roll up into a sausage shape, twisting the ends of the paper to seal. Chill in the ice compartment or freezer until firm.

Heat the remaining butter with the oil in a large shallow pan. Add 3 of the chicken escalopes and fry for 4 minutes. Turn the escalopes and fry for a further 4 minutes until golden brown and tender.

Remove the cooked escalopes to a warmed serving dish and keep warm while you fry the remaining 3 escalopes in the same way. Top each escalope with slices of the chilled parsley and garlic butter and serve immediately.

Cherries jubilee

Metric
2 × 425 g cans black cherries
4 × 15 ml spoons redcurrant
    jelly
juice and coarsely grated
    rind of 1 orange
3 × 15 ml spoons brandy
double or whipping cream,
    whipped, to serve

Imperial
2 × 15 oz cans black cherries
4 tablespoons redcurrant
    jelly
juice and coarsely grated
    rind of 1 orange
3 tablespoons brandy
double or whipping cream,
    whipped, to serve

Drain the cherries and put them into a bowl. Measure 6 × 15 ml spoons/6 tablespoons of the cherry juice and put into a shallow pan with the redcurrant jelly, and the orange juice and rind. Stir over a gentle heat until the jelly has dissolved.

Add the brandy and the cherries, and bring quickly to the boil. Carefully set light to the surface of the juice, and shake the pan gently until the flames die down. Arrange the cherries in individual glass bowls and cover with juice. Serve immediately, accompanied by whipped cream.

menu for 4

Taramasalata
"
Beef steaks with Roquefort sauce
spinach
pan-fried potatoes
"
Grapefruit sorbet

Taramasalata

Metric	Imperial
225 g smoked cod's roe	8 oz smoked cod's roe
juice of 1 lemon	juice of 1 lemon
200 ml olive oil	⅓ pint olive oil
2 garlic cloves, peeled	2 garlic cloves, peeled
2-3 ×15 ml spoons boiling water	2-3 tablespoons boiling water
freshly ground black pepper	freshly ground black pepper

To garnish:	To garnish:
4 black olives	4 black olives
sprigs of parsley	sprigs of parsley

Soak the cod's roe in cold water for 2 hours to remove some of the saltiness and to soften it. Rinse the roe, then peel off the skin. Liquidize the roe with the lemon juice, 4×15 ml spoons/4 tablespoons of the oil and the garlic until smooth. Add the remaining oil very slowly through the top of the liquidizer, until it has all been absorbed. Thin to the desired consistency with boiling water, and season with pepper.

Spoon the mixture into 4 individual shallow dishes and garnish with olives and parsley. Serve with fingers of hot toast.

Preparation the day before:
Make the Taramasalata and chill it.
Marinate the beef steaks.
Par-boil the potatoes in their skins. Remove the skins once cooked, slice, and toss in oil. Store in a covered container in the refrigerator.
Make the Grapefruit Sorbet.

One hour before dinner:
Prepare and start cooking the steaks.
Cook 1 kg/2 lb fresh spinach or 2×225 g/8 oz packets frozen spinach, pan-fry the potatoes and keep warm.
Make the Roquefort sauce.
Make toast to serve with the Taramasalata. Remove the Taramasalata from the refrigerator 30 minutes before serving.

How to make the menu serve 6
Taramasalata: hollow 6 large tomatoes and fill with the Taramasalata. Garnish with black olives and sprigs of fresh parsley.
Beef steaks with Roquefort sauce: cut the marinated steaks into thin slices crossways. Instead of cooking in the oven, fry the sliced steak in a shallow frying pan for 3 to 4 minutes, then continue with the recipe. Cut each toast croûton into 4 and arrange around the edge of the serving dish.
Vegetables: mix the drained cooked spinach with 200 ml/⅓ pint coating white sauce. Mix the pan-fried potatoes with 2 thinly sliced fried onions.
Grapefruit sorbet: spoon the sorbet into tall stemmed glasses and surround with canned grapefruit segments, well drained.

Beef steaks with Roquefort sauce

Metric	Imperial
4 large slices of bread	4 large slices of bread
4 fillet steaks, 5 cm thick	4 fillet steaks, 2 inches thick
200 ml red wine	⅓ pint red wine
few parsley stalks	few parsley stalks
1 medium onion, peeled and thinly sliced	1 medium onion, peeled and thinly sliced
2 small garlic cloves, crushed	2 small garlic cloves, crushed
2×15 ml spoons oil	2 tablespoons oil
salt	salt
freshly ground black pepper	freshly ground black pepper
75 g butter	3 oz butter
200 ml single cream	⅓ pint single cream
100 g Roquefort cheese, crumbled	4 oz Roquefort cheese, crumbled
2×15 ml spoons brandy	2 tablespoons brandy

Oven: 190°C, 375°F, Gas Mark 5

Cut the bread slices into ovals, toast them and set on one side.

Put the steaks into a shallow dish. Add the red wine, parsley stalks, onion, garlic, oil, and salt and pepper. Cover the dish with cling wrap and chill overnight in the refrigerator.

Remove the steaks from the marinade. Melt the butter in an ovenproof dish, add the steaks and turn them in the butter. Cook the steaks in a preheated oven for 10 minutes. Turn and cook for a further 10 minutes (for 'medium' done steaks). Keep the steaks warm on a serving dish.

Strain the marinade into a pan and boil briskly until reduced by one third. Add the cream and the Roquefort cheese and stir over a gentle heat until creamy. Stir in the brandy and any meat sediment left from cooking the steaks. Arrange each steak on a toast croûton and spoon the sauce over the top.

Grapefruit sorbet

Metric	Imperial
750 ml water	1¼ pints water
175 g granulated sugar	6 oz granulated sugar
grated rind and juice of 3 large grapefruit	grated rind and juice of 3 large grapefruit
2 egg whites	2 egg whites

Put the water into a pan with the sugar and grated grapefruit rind. Stir over a gentle heat until the sugar has dissolved. Increase the heat and boil gently for 20 minutes without stirring. Strain the grapefruit syrup and add the grapefruit juice. Pour into a shallow container and freeze until 'slushy'.

Tip the sorbet into a bowl and beat with a wooden spoon to break up the ice crystals. Beat the egg whites until stiff and fold them into the sorbet. Return the mixture to the container and re-freeze until firm.

Serve in scoops. To decorate, if liked, dip mint leaves into beaten egg white, then dust with caster sugar.

Prawns with lemon mayonnaise

Metric	Imperial
2 egg yolks	2 egg yolks
grated rind and juice of 1 lemon	grated rind and juice of 1 lemon
300 ml olive oil	½ pint olive oil
2×15 ml spoons finely chopped parsley	2 tablespoons finely chopped parsley
salt	salt
freshly ground black pepper	freshly ground black pepper
450 g unpeeled prawns	1 lb unpeeled prawns

Beat the egg yolks with the lemon rind and juice. Gradually whisk in the oil, in a fine trickle, until all the oil has been absorbed. If the mayonnaise is too thick, thin it with a little hot water. Stir in the parsley and salt and pepper to taste.

Half fill shallow glass bowls with crushed ice and arrange the prawns on top. Serve with the lemon mayonnaise.

Preparation the day before:
Make the lemon mayonnaise.
Make a vinaigrette dressing for the salad.
Make the Chinese Gooseberry Fruit Salad.
Cook the Chicken Provençal and chill overnight.

One hour before dinner:
Cook the savoury rice and keep warm in a serving dish – fry finely chopped onion in oil, add rice and chicken stock, cover and cook until the rice is tender and the liquid absorbed.
Make a walnut salad: mix lettuce, watercress and coarsely chopped walnuts and toss with vinaigrette.
Heat the Chicken Provençal through in a covered pan on top of the stove, while making the first course.

How to make the menu serve 6
Prawns with lemon mayonnaise: shell the prawns. Hard-boil 4 eggs, chop and mix with the prawns and lemon mayonnaise. One-third fill tall glasses with shredded lettuce and top with the mayonnaise.
Chicken provençal: remove the cooked chicken from the bone in fairly large pieces and return to the sauce. Add a small can red peppers, sliced; heat through.
Vegetables: cook extra rice.
Chinese gooseberry fruit salad: add 2 thinly sliced bananas or a can of drained mandarin oranges.

Chicken provencal

Metric	Imperial
4 chicken joints	4 chicken joints
seasoned flour	seasoned flour
2 medium onions, peeled and sliced	2 medium onions, peeled and sliced
4×15 ml spoons oil	4 tablespoons oil
2 green peppers, cored, seeded and sliced	2 green peppers, cored, seeded and sliced
2 garlic cloves, crushed	2 garlic cloves, crushed
350 g tomatoes, roughly chopped	12 oz tomatoes, roughly chopped
450 ml red wine	¾ pint red wine
200 ml chicken stock	⅓ pint chicken stock
1×5 ml spoon dried oregano	1 teaspoon dried oregano
1 bay leaf	1 bay leaf
50 g pitted black olives, to garnish	2 oz pitted black olives, to garnish

Dust the chicken joints in the seasoned flour. Fry the onions gently in the oil in a large shallow pan for 3 minutes. Add the chicken joints and fry until lightly golden all over. Add the remaining ingredients, except the black olives, then cover and simmer gently for 40 minutes. Spoon on to a warm serving dish and garnish with the black olives.

Chinese gooseberry fruit salad

Metric	Imperial
150 ml orange juice	¼ pint orange juice
juice of 1 fresh lime, or 2×15 ml spoons pure lime juice	juice of 1 fresh lime, or 2 tablespoons pure lime juice
4×15 ml spoons sweet sherry	4 tablespoons sweet sherry
6 Chinese gooseberries	6 Chinese gooseberries
1×15 ml spoon chopped pistachio nuts (optional)	1 tablespoon chopped pistachio nuts (optional)

To serve:
whipped cream
ginger to taste

To serve:
whipped cream
ginger to taste

Mix the orange juice, lime juice and sherry together. Peel the Chinese gooseberries very thinly, and cut into thin slices. Put the sliced fruit into a shallow serving dish and spoon the fruit juice and sherry mixture over the top. Cover the dish with cling film and chill overnight. Sprinkle with the chopped pistachios, and serve with whipped cream flavoured with ginger.

Variation
Use 4 ripe peaches instead of gooseberries, and lemon juice instead of lime.

Index